Texas
PROMULGATED FORMS

SECOND EDITION UPDATE

Peggy Santmyer, Contributing Author

This publication is designed to provide accurate and authoritative information in regard to the subject matter covered. It is sold with the understanding that the publisher is not engaged in rendering legal, accounting, or other professional advice. If legal advice or other expert assistance is required, the services of a competent professional should be sought.

President: Dr. Andrew Temte
Chief Learning Officer: Dr. Tim Smaby
Executive Director, Real Estate Education: Melissa Kleeman-Moy
Development Editor: Julia Marti

TEXAS PROMULGATED FORMS SECOND EDITION UPDATE
©2016 Kaplan, Inc.
Published by DF Institute, Inc., d/b/a Dearborn Real Estate Education
332 Front St. S., Suite 501
La Crosse, WI 54601

Printed in the United States of America

ISBN: 978-1-4754-0909-3

Contents

Preface

■ ABOUT THE BOOK

When representing buyers and sellers, one of the most important things a real estate licensee does is prepare and review offers for the parties by filling in the blanks of promulgated forms.

In order to be knowledgeable, as required by the Canons of Professional Ethics, it is necessary for licensees to not only know what goes in the blank, but also what is in the preprinted portion of the contract.

Licensees may not give legal advice and must advise the parties to seek help from attorneys if a question arises regarding legal rights or remedies.

Licensees can, however, point out to the parties the verbiage in the contract form. To fulfill that roll, licensees must be completely familiar with the forms.

At the conclusion of this course, you will be able to

- select the correct form or forms that are appropriate to define the agreement of the parties to a real estate transaction;
- complete promulgated forms and addenda to accurately set forth the wishes and intents of the parties;
- summarize the business details covered in the contract;
- explain how and when to use an amendment or an addendum;
- identify notices and their roles;
- describe the unauthorized practice of law and how to avoid it;
- identify potential legal problems and know when to encourage parties to seek legal advice; and
- explain the parties' options under the contract.

How to Use *Texas Promulgated Forms Supplement*

This textbook comes with the *Texas Promulgated Forms Supplement*. The supplement contains the Texas Real Estate Commission (TREC) forms discussed in this book. The forms are available on the Texas Real Estate Commission's website at http://trec.state.tx.us/formslawscontracts/forms/forms-contracts.asp (or go to http://trec.state.tx.us/, click the Forms, Laws & Contracts tab, and then click the Contract Forms and Addenda link).

As you read through this book, look up the form in the supplement and carefully read the language in it. Thoughtful study of these forms will ensure success on the exam and in your real estate practice. For ease of use, all forms are listed in the table of contents of *Texas Promulgated Forms Supplement*. Refer to the contents page for the location of the form. The forms are provided in the supplement according to the form's type (promulgated contract, promulgated addenda, approved form, etc.) and in the same order they are listed in this book under the Use of Promulgated Forms section in Chapter 2.

There are case studies/practice transactions in this book in Chapters 5, 6, and 9. The forms needed for those activities are in the supplement in the Case Studies section. You will fill out the forms according to the scenario transaction in this book. When you have filled them out entirely, you can check them against the filled-out forms that appear immediately after the blank forms for that case study.

■ WE'D LIKE TO HEAR FROM YOU

We like to hear from our readers. You are our partners in the real estate education process. Comments about this text or any services we provide are always appreciated and should be directed to *contentinquiries@dearborn.com*.

CHAPTER
1

Contract Law Overview

■ **LEARNING OBJECTIVES**   *When you have completed this chapter, you will be able to*

- ■ **identify** the essential elements of a valid contract;
- ■ **explain** the difference in valid, void, voidable, and unenforceable contracts;
- ■ **distinguish** between bilateral and unilateral, and executed and executory contracts;
- ■ **distinguish** between an amendment and an addendum, and describe how and when they are used;
- ■ **state** the statute of limitations for written and oral contracts in Texas; and
- ■ **list** reasons for a termination of a contract, including breach of contract.

■ KEY TERMS

addendum	executory contract	performance
amendment	forbearance	reasonable time
assignment	fraud	rescission
attorney-in-fact	incompetent party	Statute of Frauds
bilateral contract	lawful objective	time is of the essence
binding	legal description	unenforceable
breach	liquidated damages	unilateral contract
competent party	minor	valid
consideration	mutual agreement	void
default	novation	voidable
earnest money	option	
enforceable contract	option to purchase	
executed contract	option to terminate	

■ ELEMENTS OF A VALID CONTRACT

Every day, individuals enter into agreements to do or to refrain from doing specific acts. Some of these agreements can be classified as contracts, while others are simply agreements. A contract is a legally enforceable agreement to do (**performance**) or not to do (**forbearance**) a specific thing. Texas statutes protect contractual rights. Those who enter a contract and fail to perform (**default** or **breach**) may be sued by the other party or parties to the agreement. The non-defaulting party may ask the court to enforce specific performance or may try to prove to the court that economic damages were created by the default and seek money damages to compensate the loss.

To be considered a legally **binding** or **enforceable contract**, the agreement must meet certain requirements defined by Texas statutes. Parties who enter into agreements that do not meet those requirements may not have legal recourse when the other party decides to ignore the terms and conditions of the agreement. While a contract is legally enforceable in a court of law, an agreement may not be. When creating contracts, the final agreement should be clear, and the promises exchanged should be definite and specific.

The six elements of a valid real estate contract include the following:

- Competent parties
- Consideration
- Mutual agreement (mutual assent)
- Lawful objective
- In writing and signed by the parties
- Contain a legal description

Competent Parties

A party who does not have legal capacity (**incompetent party**) may not be held to the terms of an agreement. To be a legally **competent party**, one must have attained the age of majority, which is 18 in Texas. An individual younger than 18 may be emancipated by a court of competent jurisdiction and declared an adult with contractual capacity. A contract signed by a **minor** (younger than 18) is classified as voidable; that is, it can be set aside at the sole option of the minor party. If the minor chooses to uphold and fulfill the terms of the agreement, the contract is binding. The parties must be in control of their mental faculties. Individuals are considered sane or mentally competent until declared otherwise by a court. The parties must also be sober and demonstrate contractual intent. In short, a competent party is a person who is at least 18 years old, sane, and sober.

Any person who meets the competent party test may, through a duly executed specific power of attorney, name and appoint another to act as an attorney-in-fact. The **attorney-in-fact** serves in a fiduciary capacity to the person who makes the appointment. The signature of the attorney-in-fact binds a party just as effectively as the party's own signature. It should be noted that a power of attorney granting authority to transfer title to real property must recite the legal description of the subject of the authority.

Licensees dealing with corporate-owned real estate should remember that only an officer named in a corporate resolution, passed at a meeting of the board of directors, may sign a contract for and on behalf of the corporation. It may be a waste of a licensee's time to attempt to market and negotiate corporately owned real estate prior to obtaining a copy of the corporate resolution for the licensee's file, and subsequently, for the title company that will be asked to close the transaction.

Consideration

To be valid, a contract must identify that something, usually money, is being given in exchange for something else. Texas courts have ruled that a promise given in exchange for a promise is adequate **consideration** to bind a purchase agreement. The promise to sell and the promise to purchase, in paragraph 1 of the promulgated forms, serve as adequate consideration to bind the contract: "Your promise exchanged for my promise is a thing of value, something that is sacred in the eyes of the courts."

Many people incorrectly believe that **earnest money** must be tendered to create a valid contract. This belief was undoubtedly fostered by the fact that licensees used to refer to real estate sales contracts as earnest money contracts. With regard to a purchase contract, the listing broker best fulfills the fiduciary duty to the seller by encouraging a substantial amount of earnest money. The earnest money can demonstrate the buyer's serious intent to purchase and may serve as liquidated damages in the event of a breach of contract, as defined in paragraph 15 of the contracts promulgated by the Texas Real Estate Commission (TREC). **Liquidated damages** are monies paid to a non-defaulting party under the terms of a contract as opposed to money damages, which are determined and awarded by a court.

The one type of contract that requires a prospect to tender money to bind the agreement is an **option** contract—an option to purchase or an option to terminate. In an option contract, the property owner gives a promise and the purchaser gives money to purchase a legal right and to bind the agreement.

Mutual Agreement (Mutual Assent)

Mutual agreement means that the parties must enter the contract freely and voluntarily. Their decisions must be based on truthful, accurate information. The presence of false information or **fraud** (a deliberate act of deception) by either acts of commission (telling a lie) or acts of omission (failing to reveal material facts about the property) precludes an enforceable agreement. Licensees should take decisive action to ensure that full disclosure is made and that the parties to a purchase agreement are making their decisions based on truthful, accurate information.

Lawful Objective

Lawful objective concerns the provisions of an agreement, which must call for lawful activity. A provision that does not comply with federal, state, or local law cannot be upheld by a court. Suppose a tenant signs a lease stating that if the tenant fails to pay the rent, the landlord may enter the premises, seize all of the tenant's personal possessions, and immediately sell them to satisfy the rent obligation. Because this provision is in violation of the homestead law, it is void.

In Writing and Signed by the Parties

The **Statute of Frauds** requires that, to be enforceable, all agreements affecting title to or interest in real estate in Texas be in writing and signed by the parties. An oral agreement of sale is void and therefore unenforceable. It is inadvisable for licensees to conduct real estate negotiations orally. Offers and counteroffers should always be in writing. One does not have a binding executory contract until (1) a written offer has been made; (2) a written acceptance has occurred; and (3) the offeror has been notified of the acceptance. The only exception to the *in writing* rule is a lease for one year or less. All other real estate agreements must be in writing to be enforceable.

Contain a Legal Description

A street address does not constitute an adequate description of the property for contract and conveyance purposes. The Statute of Frauds calls for the agreement to contain a **legal description** that is of such certainty and accuracy that one can go to and identify it. The two commonly used legal descriptions are (1) reference to a recorded plat (lot, block, section number, subdivision name); and (2) metes and bounds. If students of real estate and readers of this book have not previously taken a Principles of Real Estate course, they will learn a great deal about legal descriptions if and when they do.

■ VALID/VOID/UNENFORCEABLE/VOIDABLE

If an agreement has all six of the elements described previously, it is considered **valid** and will be upheld by Texas courts. If it does not have the elements, it is identified as a **void** (the absence of) contract. Due to a change in the law or the passage of time, a contract or certain provisions of a contract may become unenforceable. It is important to emphasize that there is a difference between void and unenforceable. A void contract is not a contract at all; *void* means the absence of something. An **unenforceable** contract is an agreement that had all six elements at the time it became an executory contract but, due to a change in conditions, no longer meets the requirements of law and no longer can be upheld by a court. A void contract was never enforceable; an unenforceable contract was valid but is no longer.

As mentioned earlier, contracts can also be **voidable** (set aside at the option of one of the contracting parties). Voidable contracts typically exist in the following instances:

- When entered into with a minor, the agreement is voidable at the option of the minor party.
- When fraud by acts of commission or acts of omission can be proven, the agreement is voidable at the option of the non-fraudulent party.
- When the seller fails to provide and the buyer of a previously occupied single-family residence fails to receive the written seller's disclosure of property condition as required by section 5.008 of the Texas Property Code (and addressed in TREC Form OP-H, Seller's Disclosure of Property Condition), the contract may be terminated at the sole option of the buyer and is therefore voidable by the buyer. If the form is presented after the agreement is signed, the buyer may terminate the contract within seven days after receipt of the disclosure.
- When homeowners association information and the TREC Condominium Resale Certificate have not been provided to the buyer prior to creating an executory contract to purchase, the buyer has the unrestricted right to terminate the agreement per section 5.012 of the Texas Property Code.
- When the property is situated in a utility district or other statutorily created district providing water, sewer, drainage, or flood control, chapter 49 of the Texas Water Code establishes the contract voidable by the buyer if the seller has not forwarded the appropriate notice prior to creating an executory contract to purchase.

■ EXECUTED AND EXECUTORY CONTRACTS

When an offeror has presented a written offer, the offeree has accepted the offer in writing, and the offeror has been notified of the acceptance, an executed (signed by both parties) or enforceable contract exists.

Generally, the parties have agreed to perform all acts decided on in the agreement within 15 to 20 days and to go to closing. When all acts have been performed, the seller has delivered the general warranty deed, and the buyer has accepted it, the contract will become fully executed.

An **executory contract** is generally defined as an enforceable contract that is in the process of being performed or fulfilled. In 2005, the Texas legislature defined an executory contract as one that involves the sale of a residence in which closing will occur more than 180 days after the execution (signing by both parties) of the contract. In Texas, *executory* is a term limited in meaning to include only a contract-for-deed (also known as a land sales contract), lease-purchase, or lease-option transaction. Do not attempt to create an executory contract with any of the TREC-promulgated forms. Neither TREC, nor any real estate trade association in Texas, drafts standard forms to be used as executory contracts. Always refer customers or clients to a competent real estate attorney to draft an executory contract.

When closing and funding occur, the contract is considered a fully **executed contract**. An executory contract is one that is fully negotiated and signed by the parties. The parties still have obligations to fulfill before all things decided on in the agreement have been performed. A fully executed contract is one in which all parties have fulfilled all promises made in the agreement. When the seller has delivered the deed, received the proceeds, and granted possession to the purchaser, a fully executed contract exists.

The term *executed* may also be used informally to identify an agreement that has been signed by all parties. At the signature line on page 8 of the TREC-promulgated forms, the wording calls for the broker to enter the effective date of the contract after all parties have signed, as seen in the following:

EXECUTED the _____ day of _____, 20____ (EFFECTIVE DATE).

(BROKER: FILL IN THE DATE OF FINAL ACCEPTANCE.)

■ BILATERAL VERSUS UNILATERAL

Purchase contracts are **bilateral contracts** that involve a promise in exchange for a promise. The offer becomes valid and binding when acceptance is communicated. The seller in a purchase agreement agrees to deliver clear title, and the buyer agrees to deliver money. A **unilateral contract** involves a promise in exchange for an act. The seller agrees to pay the listing broker when and if the broker produces a ready, willing, and able buyer.

Understanding what binds whom to what and when is very important. A bilateral contract binds both parties to do or to refrain from doing specific acts starting the moment all have signed. Most real estate-related contracts are bilateral agreements. Examples of bilateral and unilateral contracts include, but are not limited to, the following:

- Independent contractor agreement—a bilateral agreement that defines the working relationship between salesperson and sponsoring broker
- Lease—a bilateral agreement that defines what the tenant may and may not do during the term of the leasehold, and what the property owner may and may not do during the term of the leasehold
- **Option to purchase**—a unilateral agreement that binds the property owner and prevents them from selling the property to another party, but does not bind the prospective purchaser to purchase
- **Option to terminate**—a unilateral agreement that binds the property owner to release the prospective purchaser from all obligations if the purchaser elects to walk away during the defined option period

■ Listing agreement—may be either a unilateral agreement or a bilateral agreement, although most listing agreements are for an exclusive-right-to-sell agency and involve an exchange of promises and obligations (only a nonexclusive or open listing may be a unilateral agreement)

■ Buyer representation agreement—a bilateral agreement that defines the working relationship between a buyer and the buyer's agent, and creates an exclusive agency relationship

■ Purchase agreement—always a bilateral agreement that calls for each of the parties to perform certain actions and/or fulfill certain promises defined in the agreement

■ REASONABLE TIME VERSUS TIME IS OF THE ESSENCE

With regard to time frames established in contracts, Texas courts always favor upholding the provisions of a contract when the parties have acted in good faith and have performed within a **reasonable time**. The court must hold the parties to exact performance within the time specified when the agreement has incorporated the words *time is of the essence*, or when an Option to Purchase or an Option to Terminate is the contract being interpreted. As you examine the text of the TREC-promulgated forms, you will find that only the Option to Terminate paragraph in the six promulgated contract forms includes *time is of the essence*. In addition, four addenda include *time is of the essence*: Addendum for Sale of Other Property by Buyer, Addendum for Back-Up Contract, Third Party Financing Addendum, and Short Sale Addendum.

A real estate broker or salesperson should never add the words *time is of the essence* to a contract or advise a customer or client to do so. If a party wants to add the words, that party and the other party should be advised to seek the counsel of a competent real estate attorney before doing so.

The TREC-promulgated contracts call for things to occur within a certain number of days after the effective date of the contract. The effective date is filled in above the signature lines by the broker after the last party, usually the seller, has signed, and the other party, usually the buyer, has been notified of the acceptance. It is very difficult to establish performance and nonperformance when a careless licensee fails to fill in the appropriate date before opening title. In fact, such carelessness can result in a significant dispute between the parties. The effective date will need to be established by the parties or perhaps by a court, if the parties cannot agree.

It is important to note that all 365 days of the year (366 days in leap year) have equal status. Just as important is that the word *after* does not include the effective day of the contract. Therefore, if the effective date of the contract is June 14, and the time frame calls for seven days, the time period will end at midnight on June 21.

■ AMENDMENTS AND ADDENDA

An amendment is completed after a contract has been executed, but addenda are completed at the same time as the sales contract.

An **amendment** is a change or modification to the existing content of a contract. Any time words or provisions are added to or deleted from the body of the contract, the contract has been amended. For instance, a form contract's provision requiring closing in 90 days might be amended to a 60-day period. TREC provides a promulgated amendment form for use. Other things that may be amended with the TREC form are the sales price, repairs to be done, seller's agreement to pay a portion of buyer's closing costs, and extension of the option to terminate period, among others. Amendments must be signed by all parties. Once a contract form has been signed and agreed upon, the proper way to make changes is with the promulgated amendment form. Used properly, the original agreement, and the date that it happened, is reflected in the contract. Each change, and the date the change happened, is reflected in the amendment.

An **addendum** contains additional information that is part of the original contract/agreement. All addenda must be listed in the Agreement of the Parties paragraph in the TREC-promulgated contract form. If TREC provides a promulgated addendum that addresses a situation, the addendum must be used. It is a violation of TREC Rules for a licensee to write something in Special Provisions if TREC has an addendum that addresses the situation. An addendum must be signed by all parties. TREC promulgates a number of addenda that are addressed throughout this book and in Chapter 7.

■ PERFORMANCE OF A CONTRACT

Each party has certain rights and duties to fulfill. The question of when a contract must be performed is an important factor. Many contracts call for a specific time by which the agreed acts must be completely performed. Furthermore, some contracts provide that time is of the essence. A party who fails to perform on time is liable for breach of contract.

Many obligations in the TREC contract forms are to be accomplished within a certain number of days after the effective date. It is very important for licensees to complete the date in the form that follows the parties' signatures (EXECUTED THE ___DAY OF ____, 20___ [EFFECTIVE DATE]). Even though the form indicates that the broker is to complete the date, most brokers have authorized their affiliated licensees to do that for them. The effective date happens immediately when both parties have agreed on everything in the written, signed contract and that acceptance has been communicated to the other party or the other party's agent. Without an effective date, there is no specific date for performance.

When a contract does not specify a date for performance, the acts it requires should be performed within a reasonable time. The interpretation of what constitutes a reasonable time depends on the situation. Courts have sometimes declared contracts to be invalid because they did not contain a time or date for performance.

Assignment and Novation

Assignment refers to a transfer of rights or duties under a contract. A party may transfer interest to another legal entity unless prohibited by statute or written agreement of the parties. Purchase contracts are typically assignable. Leases, by statute, may not be assigned without the express written permission of the property owner. Most other real estate-related contracts may be assigned unless specific language prohibiting assignment has been included in the body of the agreement. The assignor is the party who transfers a right, and the assignee is the party to whom the right is assigned. The assignee takes on all of the rights and obligations of the contract being assigned. However, the assignor is not released from the obligations of the contract. A good example is the obligation of paying back money borrowed for the purchase of a property. When a new borrower assumes the existing loan obligation, the original borrower is not discharged of his obligations unless specifically released from the obligation by the lender. Of course, the loan documents may prohibit assumption; one must always examine the loan documents to determine if the obligations may be assigned.

The replacement of an existing contract with a new contract is known as a **novation**. The new contract must reference the contract that is being replaced. There can also be a novation of the parties. A novation releases all of the terms and obligations of the original agreement.

Statute of Limitations

Every state limits the time during which parties to a contract may bring legal suit to enforce their rights. The statute of limitations varies for different legal actions, and any rights not enforced within the applicable time period are lost. In Texas, the statute of limitations for filing a legal suit on a written contract is four years. Remember that the statute of frauds requires agreements affecting title to or interest in real estate in Texas to be in writing to be enforceable, so the statute of limitations on a contract for the sale of real estate is four years.

Under the statute of frauds, leases for one year or less do not have to be in writing. An oral contract for the lease of a property for one year or less has a statute of limitation of two years.

If one of the parties defaults under the contract and the other party chooses to sue that party for specific performance and/or damages, that lawsuit must be filed within the statute of limitations time period (*see* paragraph 15 in the One to Four Family Residential Contract). If one of the parties accepts the earnest money as liquidated damages, everyone from the contract is released and no further action can be taken.

In this case the statute of limitations applies not from the date of the contract, but from the date the buyers discover the problem.

The statute of limitations also applies to disclosure issues. For example, a sale took place in 2012, and in 2013 the buyers discovered that the home had a foundation issue. When the buyer called a structural engineer to inspect the foundation, the engineer told the buyer that he had been to the property before. He told the sellers that they needed piers when he was there in 2011, and the work had never been done. The buyers reviewed the seller's disclosure, received at the time they purchased the property, and verified that the seller had not disclosed a problem with the foundation. The buyers consulted an attorney who told them they were well within the statute of limitations, which begins at the time the problem is discovered (the time the buyers discovered the problem). The buyers and their attorney decided to pursue a lawsuit against the seller for the amount of the foundation repairs.

■ REASONS FOR TERMINATION

A contract is discharged when the agreement is terminated. The most desirable case is when a contract terminates because it was completely performed, with all its terms fulfilled. Contracts may be terminated for other reasons, such as a party's breach or default.

Breach of Contract

A contract may be terminated if it is breached by one of the parties. A breach of contract is a violation of any of the terms or conditions of a contract without legal reason. A seller who fails to deliver title to the buyer breaches a sales contract. The breaching or defaulting party assumes certain burdens, and the non-defaulting party has certain legal remedies.

If the seller breaches a real estate sales contract, the buyer may sue for specific performance unless the contract specifically states otherwise. In a suit for specific performance, the buyer asks the court to force the seller to go through with the sale and transfer the property as previously agreed. The buyer may choose to sue for damages, in which case the seller is asked to pay for any costs and hardships suffered by the buyer as a result of the seller's breach.

If the buyer defaults, the seller can sue for damages or sue for the purchase price. A suit for the purchase price is essentially a suit for specific performance. The seller tenders the deed and asks that the buyer be required to pay the agreed price.

The contract may limit the remedies available to the parties. A liquidated damages clause in a real estate purchase contract specifies the amount of money the seller is entitled to if the buyer breaches the contract.

The TREC-promulgated contracts designate the earnest money as liquidated damages if one of the parties breaches the contract. Once one of the parties accepts the earnest money as liquidated damages, everyone is released from the contract with no further remedies.

Other Reasons for Termination

Contracts may also be discharged or terminated when one of the following occurs:

■ Partial performance of the terms—including a written acceptance by the party for whom acts have not been done or to whom money is owed. For instance, if the parties agree that the work performed is close enough to completion, they can agree that the contract is discharged even if some minor elements remain unperformed.

■ Substantial performance—in which one party has substantially performed on the contract but does not complete all the details exactly as the contract requires. Such performance may be enough to force payment, with certain adjustments for any damages suffered by the other party. For example, where a newly constructed addition to a home is finished except for polishing the brass doorknobs, the contractor is entitled to the final payment.

■ Impossibility of performance—in which an act required by the contract cannot be legally accomplished.

■ Mutual agreement— the parties agree to cancel the contract.

■ Operation of law—as a result of fraud, due to the expiration of the statute of limitations, or because a contract was altered without the written consent of all parties involved. This includes the voiding of a contract by a minor.

■ Rescission—one party cancels or terminates the contract as though it had never been made. Cancellation terminates a contract without a return to the original position. **Rescission**, however, returns the parties to their original positions before the contract, so any monies exchanged must be returned. Rescission is normally a contractual remedy for a breach, but a contract may also be rescinded by the mutual agreement of the parties.

■ SUMMARY

To be considered a legally binding or enforceable contract, the agreement must meet certain requirements defined by Texas statute.

The elements of a valid contract include competent parties, consideration, a valid legal description, mutual agreement, lawful objective, in writing, and signed by the parties.

Contracts can be valid, void, unenforceable, or voidable.

A contract may be executed (all parties have fulfilled their promises) or executory (one or both parties still have an act to perform). Real estate licensees may not prepare the forms for executory contracts such as contracts for deed or lease options. These forms must be prepared by an attorney.

A contract may be bilateral (having obligations on both sides) or unilateral (a promise by one side that can be accepted or rejected by the other side).

An amendment is a change or modification to the existing content of a contract. An addendum is any provision added to a contract as part of the original agreement.

The statute of limitations for a written contract is four years.

Contracts may be discharged (completed) by the following:

■ Performance, which completes the contract terms
■ Partial performance, if agreeable to both parties

- Substantial performance, depending on circumstances
- Impossibility of performance (required acts cannot be legally accomplished)
- Assignment (transfer of rights to assignee or delegation of duties)
- Novation (substitutes a new contract or party for the original)
- Breach by one of the parties without legal cause
- Liquidated damages clause may specify the amount the seller will receive if the buyer defaults
- Failure to enforce contract within statute of limitations
- Mutual agreement of parties
- Operation of law, as when a contract is void from inception
- Rescission (cancellation) by one or both parties

CHAPTER 1 QUIZ

1. Which of the following is *NOT* an essential element of a valid contract?
   a. Consideration
   b. Earnest money
   c. Mutual agreement
   d. In writing and signed by the parties

2. The law that requires the contract to be in writing and signed by the parties is the
   a. Texas Deceptive Trade Practices Act.
   b. Law of Contracts.
   c. Statute of Frauds.
   d. Fair Housing Act.

3. A contract that is unenforceable
   a. was once valid but is no longer so.
   b. was never valid.
   c. is voidable.
   d. is missing one of the elements of a valid contract.

4. An oral agreement of sale is
   a. valid.
   b. voidable.
   c. enforceable by the court.
   d. void and unenforceable.

5. A contract can be terminated at the option of the buyer when
   a. the seller fails to provide and the buyer, of a previously occupied single-family residence, fails to receive the written seller's disclosure of property condition.
   b. homeowners association information and the Condominium Resale Certificate have not been provided to the buyer prior to creating a contract to purchase.
   c. the property is situated in a utility district or other statutorily created district providing water, sewer, drainage, or flood control (chapter 49 of the Texas Water Code), and the seller has not forwarded the appropriate notice prior to creating a contract to purchase.
   d. all of these.

6. Contracts can be discharged or terminated for all of the following reasons *EXCEPT*
   a. when the buyer sends an amendment to the seller asking for a change in the closing date.
   b. if the contract is voided by a minor.
   c. when the parties agree to cancel or terminate.
   d. if the transaction is fraudulent.

7. When the parties agree to change a contract that has already been agreed upon, the proper form to use is the
   a. Addendum.
   b. Notice to Buyer.
   c. Amendment.
   d. Termination Agreement.

8. A document that transfers contract obligations to another party but does *NOT* release the first party's obligation is
   a. a novation.
   b. an assignment.
   c. an amendment.
   d. an addendum.

9. Once the duties in a contract are completed by both parties, the contract is
   a. unilateral.
   b. bilateral.
   c. executed.
   d. executory.

10. A sales contract in which a promise is exchanged for a promise is
    a. unilateral.
    b. executed.
    c. executory.
    d. bilateral.

CHAPTER

2

Laws, Rules, and Regulations

■ **LEARNING OBJECTIVES** *When you have completed this chapter, you will be able to*

- ■ **discuss** the role The Real Estate License Act plays in the use of promulgated forms;
- ■ **describe** the unauthorized practice of law and how to avoid it;
- ■ **describe** the composition and duties of the Broker-Lawyer Committee;
- ■ **recall** how many TREC forms there are and identify whether a TREC form is a promulgated contract, addenda, amendment, resale certificate, notice, consumer disclosure, or an approved option/voluntary use form; and
- ■ **describe** the proper procedure for presenting offers and multiple offers, and identify when the offer becomes a contract.

■ KEY TERMS

Broker-Lawyer Committee	tort	unauthorized practice of
counteroffer	TREC (Texas Real Estate	law
offer	Commission)	
promulgate	TRELA (Texas Real Estate	
	License Act)	

■ TEXAS REAL ESTATE LICENSE ACT

Real estate professionals in Texas were first licensed through the Securities Division of the Secretary of State's office, beginning in 1939 with passage of the Real Estate Dealers License Act (House Bill 17, 46th Legislature, Regular Session).

In 1949 the **Texas Real Estate Commission (TREC)** was created to administer the act (Senate Bill 28, 51st Legislature, Regular Session).

The act's name was changed to the **Texas Real Estate License Act (TRELA)** in 1955. The purpose of the **TRELA** is to protect the public through regulation of licensed real estate brokerage practitioners, real estate inspectors, residential service companies, and entities offering timeshare interests.

The policy-making body of the Texas Real Estate Commission is a nine-member commission appointed by the governor with the advice and consent of the senate for overlapping six-year terms. Six members must be active in real estate as full-time brokers for five years immediately preceding appointment. Three members must not be licensed by the commission and have no financial interest in real estate, except as consumers.

The commission has rule-making authority and the rules of the commission have the full force and effect of law. As it pertains to contract forms, that authority is established in the part of the TRELA, reproduced in the following:

> *Sec. 1101.155. RULES RELATING TO CONTRACT FORMS. (a) The commission may adopt rules in the public's best interest that require license holders to use contract forms prepared by the Texas Real Estate Broker-Lawyer Committee* [discussed later in this chapter] *and adopted by the commission.*
> *(b) The commission may not prohibit a license holder from using for sale, exchange, option, or lease of an interest in real property a contract form that is:*
> > *(1) prepared by the property owner; or*
> > *(2) prepared by an attorney and required by the property owner.*

In addition to itemizing the current inventory of available forms, the commission establishes the dos and don'ts for the completion of the forms. A careful reading of the rules tells licensees all they need to know. The underlining in the following excerpt has been added for emphasis:

> *537.11. Use of Standard Contract Forms*
> *(a) When negotiating contracts binding the sale, exchange, option, lease or rental of any interest in real property, a real estate licensee shall use only those contract forms promulgated by the Texas Real Estate Commission (the commission) for that kind of transaction with the following exceptions:*
> > *(1) transactions in which the licensee is functioning solely as a principal, not as an agent;*
> > *(2) transactions in which an agency of the United States government requires a different form to be used;*

(3) transactions for which a contract form has been prepared by a principal to the transaction or prepared by an attorney and required by a principal to the transaction; or

(4) transactions for which no standard contract form has been promulgated by the commission, and the licensee uses a form prepared by an attorney at law licensed by this state and approved by the attorney for the particular kind of transactions involved or prepared by the Texas Real Estate Broker-Lawyer Committee (the committee) and made available for trial use by licensees with the consent of the commission.

537.11 (b) and Following

(b) A licensee may not:

(1) practice law;

(2) offer, give or attempt to give legal advice, directly or indirectly;

(3) give advice or opinions as to the legal effect of any contracts or other such instruments which may affect the title to real estate;

(4) give opinions concerning the status or validity of title to real estate; or

(5) <u>attempt to prevent or in any manner whatsoever discourage any principal to a real estate transaction from employing a lawyer.</u>

(c) Nothing in this section shall be deemed to limit the licensee's fiduciary obligation to disclose to the licensee's principals all pertinent facts which are within the knowledge of the licensee, including such facts which might affect the status of or title to real estate.

(d) A licensee <u>may not undertake to draw or prepare documents fixing and defining the legal rights of the principals to a real estate transaction.</u>

(e) In negotiating real estate transactions, the licensee <u>may fill in forms for such</u> transactions, using exclusively forms which have been approved and promulgated by the commission or such forms as are otherwise permitted by these rules.

(f) When filling in a form authorized for use by this section, <u>the licensee may only fill in the blanks provided and may not add to or strike matter from such form, except that licensees shall add factual statements and business details desired by the principals</u> and shall strike only such matter as is desired by the principals and as is necessary to conform the instrument to the intent of the parties.

(g) A <u>licensee may not add to a promulgated contract form factual statements or business details for which a contract addendum, lease or other form has been promulgated by the commission for mandatory use.</u>

(h) Nothing in this section shall be deemed to prevent the licensee from explaining to the principals the meaning of the factual statements and business details contained in the said instrument so long as the licensee does not offer or give legal advice.

(i) It is not the practice of law as defined in this Act for a real estate licensee to complete a contract form which is either promulgated by the commission or prepared by the committee and made available for trial use by licensees with the consent of the commission.

(j) Contract forms prepared by the committee for trial use may be used on a voluntary basis after being approved by the commission.

(k) Contract forms prepared by the committee and approved by the commission to replace previously promulgated forms may be used by licensees

on a voluntary basis prior to the effective date of rules requiring use of the replacement form.

(l) Where it appears that, prior to the execution of any such instrument, there are unusual matters involved in the transaction which should be resolved by legal counsel before the instrument is executed or that the instrument is to be acknowledged and filed for record, the licensee shall advise the principals that each should consult a lawyer of the principal's choice before executing same.

(m) A licensee may not employ, directly or indirectly, a lawyer nor pay for the services of a lawyer to represent any principal to a real estate transaction in which the licensee is acting as an agent. The licensee may employ and pay for the services of a lawyer to represent only the licensee in a real estate transaction, including preparation of the contract, agreement, or other legal instruments to be executed by the principals to the transactions.

(n) A licensee shall advise the principals that the instrument they are about to execute is binding on them.

(o) Forms approved or promulgated by the commission may be reproduced only from the following sources:

(1) numbered copies obtained from the commission, whether in a printed format or electronically reproduced from the files available on the commission's web site;

(2) printed copies made from copies obtained from the commission;

(3) legible photocopies made from such copies; or

(4) computer-driven printers following these guidelines:

(A) The computer file or program containing the form text must not allow the end user direct access to the text of the form and may only permit the user to insert language in blanks in the forms. Blanks may be scalable to accommodate the inserted language. The commission may approve the use of a computer file or program that permits a principal of a licensee to strike through language of the form text. The program must be:

(i) limited to use only by a principal of a transaction; and

(ii) in a format and authenticated in a manner acceptable to the commission.

(B) Typefaces or fonts must appear to be identical to those used by the commission in printed copies of the particular form.

(C) The text and order of the text must be identical to that used by the commission in printed copies of the particular form.

(D) The name and address of the person or firm responsible for developing the software program must be legibly printed below the border at the bottom of each page in no less than 6 point type and in no larger than 10 point type.

(p) Forms approved or promulgated by the commission must be reproduced on the same size of paper used by the commission with the following changes or additions only.

(1) The business name or logo of a broker, organization or printer may appear at the top of a form outside the border.

(2) The broker's name may be inserted in any blank provided for that purpose.

(q) Standard Contract Forms adopted by the Commission are published by and available from the Commission at P.O. Box 12188, Austin, Texas 78711-2188 or www.trec.texas.gov.

Before engaging in the business of completing any contract forms that bind the sale, lease, temporary lease, or rental of any real property, the licensee should become thoroughly familiar with what the rules do and do not permit.

■ UNAUTHORIZED PRACTICE OF LAW

The TRELA specifically prohibits licensees from practicing law by giving opinions or counsel regarding the validity or legal sufficiency of an instrument that addresses real property rights or as to the status of title to real estate. Throughout the act, it is clearly established that, prior to signing a purchase contract, the licensee must give a buyer written advice to have the abstract covering the property examined by an attorney of the buyer's selection or to obtain an owner's title insurance policy prior to closing. Failure to give this written advice may result in disciplinary action by the TREC.

Licensees who choose to become REALTORS® subscribe to a REALTOR® Code of Ethics that demands a very high level of professional conduct. The National Association of REALTORS® Code of Ethics advises against the **unauthorized practice of law**. Again, licensees are to advise their clients/customers to seek an attorney's advice for matters that require it.

The TRELA clearly establishes that it is illegal for the licensee to draw a deed, note, deed of trust, will, or other written instrument that transfers or may transfer an interest in or title to real property. However, the act goes on to give permission for a licensee to complete a contract form that may bind the sale, exchange, option, lease, or rental of any interest in real property as long as forms are used that have been prepared by or are required by the property owner or have been provided by the real estate commission, prepared by an attorney licensed by Texas, and approved by that attorney for a particular type of transaction.

Sec. 1101.654. SUSPENSION OR REVOCATION OF LICENSE OR CERTIFICATE FOR UNAUTHORIZED PRACTICE OF LAW.
(a) The commission shall suspend or revoke the license or certificate of registration of a license or certificate holder who is not a licensed attorney in this state and who, for consideration, a reward, or in a pecuniary benefit, present or anticipated, direct or indirect, or in connection with the person's employment, agency, or fiduciary relationship as a license or certificate holder:
> *(1) drafts an instrument, other than a form described by Section 1101.155, that transfers or otherwise affects an interest in real property; or*
> *(2) advises a person regarding the validity or legal sufficiency of an instrument or the validity of title to real property.*
(b) Notwithstanding any other law, a license or certificate holder who completes a contract form for the sale, exchange, option, or lease of an interest

in real property incidental to acting as a broker is not engaged in the unauthorized or illegal practice of law in this state if the form was:
>*(1) adopted by the commission for the type of transaction for which the form is used;*
>*(2) prepared by an attorney licensed in this state and approved by the attorney for the type of transaction for which the form is used; or*
>*(3) prepared by the property owner or by an attorney and required by the property owner.*

The licensee is free to explain to the principals the meaning of the factual statements or business details contained in the contracts as long as the licensee does not offer or give legal advice.

When adding things to Special Provisions, licensees must take care that they do not cross the line and say things that change parties' legal rights. For example, saying "this contract is contingent upon a satisfactory appraisal or satisfactory inspection" changes the buyer's rights under the contract and may be the unauthorized practice of law.

Another common error is for licensees to add things to special provisions that are already in the TREC contract or on a TREC addendum. A thorough understanding of the forms will prevent issues like this.

■ THE BROKER-LAWYER COMMITTEE

One of the advisory committees that exists under the TRELA is the **Broker-Lawyer Committee.**

The committee is composed of six Real Estate Commission appointees (who are licensed real estate brokers) and six lawyers, appointed by the president of the State Bar of Texas, and one public member, appointed by the governor. They serve staggered six-year terms.

The Broker-Lawyer Committee drafts and revises contract forms for use by real estate licensees. The purpose is to expedite real estate transactions and reduce controversies while protecting the interests of the parties involved.

This Broker-Lawyer Committee, does not **promulgate**, or publish, forms for mandatory use by licensees. Only the TREC has been given rule-making authority. The Broker-Lawyer Committee develops forms and recommends their adoption, but it is the TREC that promulgates the forms for mandatory use. The act clearly establishes the membership in and responsibilities of the committee. Carefully review the following text of the act.

>*SUBCHAPTER F*
>*TEXAS REAL ESTATE BROKER-LAWYER COMMITTEE*
>*Sec. 1101.251. DEFINITION OF COMMITTEE. In this subchapter, "committee" means the Texas Real Estate Broker-Lawyer Committee.*

Sec. 1101.252. COMMITTEE MEMBERSHIP. (a) The Texas Real Estate Broker-Lawyer Committee consists of 13 members appointed as follows:

    (1) six members appointed by the commission;

    (2) six members of the State Bar of Texas appointed by the president of the state bar; and

    (3) one public member appointed by the governor.

(b) Appointments to the committee shall be made without regard to the race, creed, sex, religion, or national origin of the appointee.

Sec. 1101.254. POWERS AND DUTIES.

(a) In addition to other delegated powers and duties, the committee shall draft and revise contract forms that are capable of being standardized to expedite real estate transactions and minimize controversy.

(b) The contract forms must contain safeguards adequate to protect the principals in the transaction.

■ USE OF PROMULGATED FORMS

TREC rule 537.11 addresses the use of standardized forms and lists the forms that are currently promulgated (published) for mandatory use by a licensee when the form fits a transaction.

The Real Estate Commission has promulgated and approved these forms for licensees' use.

6   Promulgated Contracts

15   Promulgated Addenda (including two Temporary Leases)

1   Promulgated Amendment

2   Promulgated Resale Certificates

1   Promulgated Notice

2   Promulgated Consumer Disclosures

7   Approved Forms (including two approved addenda)

The promulgated forms available through TREC are listed on the following pages. The forms change regularly; visit TREC's website (click the Forms, Laws & Contracts tab) for information about current forms, including the date the form was promulgated and the current version number of the form. Earlier versions of forms may not be used; to do so could be considered the unauthorized practice of law. The version number (form number) of the form is included in the bottom right corner of each page of the form (see Figure 2.1). Pay attention to the form numbers. In addition to providing version control, it's possible you might hear a form referred to by its number instead of its name (e.g., 20-13 instead of One to Four Family Residential Contract).

Remember that you must use promulgated forms unless one of the four exceptions (*see* 537.11. Use of Standard Contract Forms on pages 15–16) comes into play.

FIGURE 2.1

One to Four Family Residential Contract Version Number

Initialed for identification by Buyer_____ _____ and Seller _____ _____   TREC NO. 20-13

Texas Real Estate Commission Forms

Promulgated Contracts:
Unimproved Property Contract
One to Four Family Residential Contract (Resale)
New Home Contract (Incomplete Construction)
New Home Contract (Completed Construction)
Farm and Ranch Contract
Residential Condominium Contract (Resale)

Promulgated Addenda:
Addendum for Sale of Other Property by Buyer
Addendum for Back-Up Contract
Addendum for Release of Liability on Assumed Loan and/or Restoration of
     Seller's VA Entitlement
Seller's Temporary Residential Lease
Buyer's Temporary Residential Lease
Seller Financing Addendum
Environmental Assessment, Threatened or Endangered Species, and Wetlands
     Addendum
Addendum for Coastal Area Property
Addendum for Property Located Seaward of the Gulf Intracoastal Waterway
Addendum for Property Subject to Mandatory Membership in an Owners' As-
     sociation
Third Party Financing Addendum
Loan Assumption Addendum
Addendum for Reservation of Oil, Gas and Other Minerals
Short Sale Addendum
Addendum to Property in a Propane Gas System Service Area

Promulgated Amendment:
Amendment to Contract

Promulgated Resale Certificates:
Condominium Resale Certificate
Subdivision Information, Including Resale Certificate for Property Subject to
     Mandatory Membership in an Owners Association

Promulgated Notice:
Notice of Buyer's Termination of Contract

Promulgated Consumer Disclosures:
Consumer Information Form 1-1
Disclosure of Relationship with Residential Service Company

Approved Optional/Voluntary Use Forms:
Notice to Prospective Buyer

Seller's Disclosure of Property Condition
Texas Real Estate Consumer Notice Concerning Hazards or Deficiencies
Information About Brokerage Services
Lead-Based Paint Addendum
Non-Realty Items Addendum

■ PRESENTING OFFERS AND MULTIPLE OFFERS

All offers should be in writing and presented to the property owner as quickly as is reasonably practical. The TREC rules call for immediate presentation. No real estate broker or salesperson has the right to withhold an offer from a property owner. To do so may result in suspension or revocation of one's license under the provisions of the TRELA or worse, result in an unpleasant lawsuit for tortious interference. A **tort** is an act that damages another individual and gives rise to legal action. A property owner may consider the licensee's failure to present an offer in a timely manner a tortious interference with the licensee's ability to sell the property.

Every licensee in Texas must successfully complete a 30-hour course in the law of agency to obtain a license. As taught in the law of agency, licensees must never lose sight of their fiduciary duties to their clients when helping them negotiate contracts. In addition to obedience (finding a buyer for the property); loyalty (putting the client's interest above all others, including the licensee's own); confidentiality (not revealing the client's personal information, although licensees have the duty to disclose all material facts about the property not specifically excluded by statute); reasonable care; and due diligence, licensees owe their clients disclosure and accounting. Failure to present an offer is certainly a breach of a licensee's fiduciary duties, as well as the possible basis for a tortious interference lawsuit. Unless instructed otherwise by the seller, all offers must be presented. A seller's instruction not to present back-up offers must be given to the licensee in writing.

A seller presented with a written offer may

- accept it,
- reject it,
- counter it, or
- do nothing (ignore it).

When an offer is unacceptable to the property owner, the owner's interest is best served when the owner gives written notice that the offer is unacceptable, thanks the offeror for the prospect's interest in the property, and invites the offeror to submit another offer. The seller should give the offeror information that will shed some light on what terms would be more acceptable to the offeree. A Realtor® and his or her client might use the Texas Association of REALTORS® (TAR) Seller's Invitation to Buyer to Submit New Offer form, available to TAR members at www.TexasREALTORS.com. The form is specifically designed for this purpose. Licensees who are not members of TAR might simply create a letter to convey the message to the offeror (*see* Figure 2.2).

FIGURE 2.2

Letter of Nonacceptance

Dear Mr. and Mrs. Cross,

Thank you for your offer to purchase our home at 4221 Pine Hollow Drive. We cannot accept your offer as presented. We appreciate your interest and encourage you to submit another offer which will be more favorably considered if you will

■ offer a purchase price more in line with current market value,
■ close within 30 to 60 days,
■ purchase the property in its present condition, and
■ pay your own loan origination costs including the fee for the survey required by your lender.

Although this is not a counteroffer, we look forward to hearing from you soon.

Sincerely,
John and Elizabeth Wagner

Note: When using this letter, do not sign the offer.

Remember, an **offer** or **counteroffer** remains open until accepted, rejected, or withdrawn. For example, if the seller has countered one offer and then a better offer comes in, the seller must be careful to withdraw his counteroffer to the first buyer before making a counteroffer to the second buyer.

A potential purchaser may withdraw an offer to purchase a property in writing anytime before the potential purchaser is notified of the offer's acceptance.

Multiple Offers

The proper handling of multiple offers is a common challenge. TREC rule 535.156 addresses this issue. TREC rule 535.156(a) specifically requires a licensee to "convey to the principal all known information which would affect the principal's decision on whether or not to accept or reject offers." Subsection 535.156(c) further provides that "a licensee has an affirmative duty to keep the principal informed at all times of significant information applicable to the transaction or transactions in which the licensee is acting as agent for the principal." Thus the rules require the listing agent to submit all written purchase offers to the seller until a buyer and the seller have a fully executed contract.

Although the general rule is that all offers must be communicated to the seller by the listing agent, there are a few exceptions. These include instances where the seller has specifically instructed the listing broker, in writing, not to bring the seller any offers below a certain price, or situations in which a binding contract has been executed between a seller and buyer. A good business practice to follow is to always have such directives reduced to writing and retained in your permanent file on the property and/or client. In the latter situation, Rule 535.156(a) provides that "the licensee shall have no duty to submit offers to the principal after the principal has accepted an offer." However, the seller may want to continue to try to negotiate a back-up offer. Be certain you know the seller's wishes going forward. Furthermore, the listing agent is discouraged from sharing any information about one buyer's offer with another buyer.

Good business practice dictates that listing agents keep other agents informed about their offers. If the seller rejects an offer, the listing agent should ask the seller to write *rejected* on the offer and sign or initial. This gives the other agent and the buyer proof that the offer was presented.

The listing should address the broker's duty regarding back-up offers to avoid confusion on the issue. Also, trade association rules and standards of practice may affect the broker's duty.

In the end, it is always the seller's decision whether to accept or reject offers they receive. The seller has no legal duty to respond to any offer and is free to consider any and all offers until an offer is accepted. The seller has no duty to respond to the offers in any particular order; if three offers are received, the seller may reject the offers that were received first and second and accept the third.

■ WHEN DOES THE OFFER BECOME A CONTRACT?

The offer becomes a contract when all parties have agreed to all terms of the offer and have signed the contract. That final date of acceptance is the date on which the contract becomes binding between the parties. The following four things must take place in order for the contract to become binding and effective (becoming the effective date in the contract):

- Be in writing
- Buyer and the seller sign final contract and initial all changes
- Acceptance is complete, without doubt
- Last party to accept communicates (can be verbal) that written acceptance has taken place to the other party (or the other party's agent)

Remember, the promulgated contract forms instruct the agent acting for the broker to fill in this final date (date of final acceptance) as the effective date. Even though the form says "BROKER: FILL IN THE DATE OF FINAL ACCEPTANCE" affiliated licensees are usually authorized by the broker to complete the effective date.

A good business practice for the licensee who obtains the final signature, or the final initial, on the contract form is to immediately call the licensee working with or for the other party to inform them that the offer is finalized and that they are now filling out the effective date. That communication should be followed up with a written copy as soon as possible.

An important thing for licensees to remember is that until this finalization occurs, the property is still for sale and any other offers must be presented. There is no such thing as "almost sold."

■ SUMMARY

Real estate in Texas is governed by the statutory laws of the state. Laws are passed by the state legislators and enforced by the TREC.

In addition to TRELA, licensees must be aware of the TREC Rules.

The Broker-Lawyer Committee drafts and edits contract forms for use by real estate licensees and TREC approves and promulgates them.

Real estate licensees must use the promulgated forms except in specific exempted cases.

Promulgated contract forms cannot be altered except as a requirement of the parties.

TREC rules contain provisions regarding the presentation of offers and multiple offers. A seller presented with a written offer has four choices: accept it, reject it, counter it, or do nothing.

An offer becomes a contract when all parties have agreed to all terms of the offer and have signed the contract.

CHAPTER 2 QUIZ

1. The purpose of the TRELA is to
   a. protect real estate licensees.
   b. protect real estate brokers from unscrupulous salespeople.
   c. protect the public.
   d. keep the cost of real estate services under control.

2. Which group administers the TRELA?
   a. Texas Real Estate Commission
   b. National Association of REALTORS®
   c. Texas Association of REALTORS®
   d. Broker-Lawyer Committee

3. The Broker-Lawyer Committee
   a. drafts and edits forms.
   b. approves forms.
   c. promulgates forms.
   d. approves and promulgates forms.

4. How many members make up the Broker-Lawyer Committee?
   a. 9
   b. 13
   c. 10
   d. 17

5. Which action might leave a licensee open to a charge of practicing law without a license?
   a. Licensee advises the seller that the property probably won't sell because it is overpriced.
   b. Licensee advises the buyer, in writing, that a title policy should be obtained as well as a survey.
   c. Licensee advises both the seller and the buyer that, in his opinion, title to the subject property is encumbered.
   d. Licensee adds factual statements and business details to a promulgated form as requested by the client.

6. The seller is
   a. obligated to accept any offer that is at or above the list price.
   b. obligated to accept any offer that will net the seller the amount she agreed upon.
   c. never obligated to accept any offer.
   d. obligated to accept any offer that has a reasonable possession date.

7. Which of the following is *TRUE* regarding the presentation of offers to a seller?
   a. A licensee can use his discretion in determining which offers to present to the seller.
   b. Licensees are not required to present offers to sellers that are 30% below the asking price.
   c. A licensee doesn't have to present offers $20,000 below the asking price if the seller has given the licensee that direction in writing.
   d. Licensees need to present all offers to sellers within one month of receiving the offer.

8. If the seller has already sent a counteroffer to a prospective buyer and then receives another offer that is even better, the seller
   a. must wait to hear from the first buyer.
   b. is free to counter this offer too.
   c. must tell the first buyer about the second offer and give them an opportunity to come up to the new amount.
   d. should withdraw the first counter before answering the new offer.

9. Which of the following is *NOT* an exception to the rules requiring that promulgated forms be used and completed by the licensee?
   a. When the contract form has been prepared by the seller's attorney and is required by the seller
   b. When an agency of the U.S. government requires a different form
   c. When the contract form has been prepared by the buyer's agent
   d. When the licensee is functioning solely as a principal

10. What should a licensee do when there are unusual matters involved in a transaction?
    a. Explain it to the best of his ability before letting the prospect sign the contract
    b. Ignore it and hope that the client understands it
    c. Have the client sign the form and then advise the client to talk to an attorney
    d. Advise the client to seek legal advice before signing anything

Parties, Property, and the Money

■ **LEARNING OBJECTIVES**   *When you have completed this chapter, you will be able to*

■ **list** the information required to complete contract forms;

■ **fill** out paragraphs 1 through 3 of the One to Four Family Residential Contract and be able to identify the provisions within them;

■ **identify** which items should be in included in the Non-Realty Items Addendum; and

■ **fill** out the financing addenda:
— Third Party Financing Addendum
— Loan Assumption Addendum
— Seller Financing Addendum
— Addendum for Release of Liability on Assumed Loan and/or Restoration of Seller's VA Entitlement

■ KEY TERMS

assumption	non-realty items	restoration of seller's
community property	parties	entitlement
legal description	release of liability	seller financing
		third party financing

■ INTRODUCTION

Unfortunately, many licensees fail to take the time to carefully read and understand the content of many of the promulgated forms before attempting to use them to capture the wishes of the party or **parties** whom they represent. This chapter identifies the most common information needed to complete the TREC-promulgated forms. In addition, starting with this chapter, we will examine the One to Four Family Residential Contract (Resale), which is the most frequently used of the TREC-promulgated forms.

■ INFORMATION NEEDED TO COMPLETE CONTRACT FORMS

The various paragraphs of the contract forms might be thought of as the building blocks of a solid transaction. The parties can choose the size and shape of the blocks to be used to build their transaction. Some of the blocks will need to be modified to create the transaction desired by the principals. The knowledgeable licensee will help the parties identify the alternatives available to them and then let the parties choose the details of their transaction. The following checklist will enable the licensee to guide the parties in the selection of the appropriate contract form for their situation and the needed addenda to clearly define the details of the transaction.

To complete paragraph 1

- Name(s) of Seller(s) as on deed or owner's title policy including marital status
- Name(s) of Buyer(s) as Buyers wish to take title; include marital status

To complete paragraph 2

- Legal description including:

    Lot number _____; Block number _____;
    Section number _____;
    Subdivision name _____
    County _____; City _____
    Address _____; Zip code _____

- Excluded fixtures and accessories _____
    _____

To complete paragraph 3

- Cash down payment $ _____
- Amount of 1st loan $ _____; 2nd loan $_____
- Sales price $_____

To complete paragraph 4

- Is the real estate license holder a party to the transaction?
- Is the real estate license holder acting on behalf of a spouse, parent, child, or business entity in which the license holder owns more than 10%?
- Is the real estate license holder a trustee for a trust where the beneficiary is the license holder's spouse, parent, or child?
- Disclose if applicable _____.

To complete paragraph 5

- Earnest money amount $_____
- Additional earnest money and date of deposit if any _____
- Escrow officer _____
- Address _____

To complete paragraph 6

- Who will pay for title policy? _____
- What company will issue the title policy? _____
- Survey: New or existing _____ Who will pay? _____
  Who will furnish? _____
- Number of days to furnish? _____
- Possible reasons for objections _____
- How many days for Buyer to raise title objections? _____
- Is property subject to mandatory membership in an HOA? _____

To complete paragraph 7

- Has Buyer received Seller's disclosure notice? _____
- If not, how many days for Seller to furnish? _____
- Was house built prior to 1978? _____
- Do you need to use the Lead Addendum? _____
- Are there specific repairs required by the Buyer? _____
  _____
  _____
- How much does the Buyer want the seller to contribute to the price of a residential service contract? $_____

To complete paragraphs 9 and 10

- By what date will closing hopefully take place? _____
- When will possession occur? _____
- If possession is before or after closing, define the terms of the temporary tenancy on the appropriate TREC temporary lease. _____
  _____
  _____

To complete paragraph 11

- Are there any business details not addressed in other parts of the contract?
  _____
  _____
  _____

To complete paragraph 12

A breakdown of both the buyer's and seller's expenses can be found in paragraph 12. Information in assisting you to estimate both the buyer's and the seller's expenses can be found in Texas Association of REALTORS® (TAR) forms 1935 and 1936.

Nonmembers may not use TAR forms; to complete paragraph 12, make a list of the items in paragraph 12 and create an estimated cost sheet for both the buyer and the seller. The title company and lenders are great sources of information. Remember, the seller must pay all of the seller expenses plus any amount agreed to pay for buyer in paragraph 12.

■ How much will Seller contribute toward Buyer's Expenses? $ _____

To complete paragraph 21

	Buyer	Seller
■ Address:	_____	_____
■ Phone numbers:	_____	_____
■ Fax number:	_____	_____
■ Email address:	_____	_____

To complete paragraph 22

■ What addenda will need to be added to the agreement? _____
_____
_____
_____
_____
_____

To complete paragraph 23

■ How much is the option fee? _____
■ How many days is the option period being purchased? _____
■ Will the option fee be credited to the Sales Price at closing? _____

To complete paragraph 24

	Buyer's Attorney	Seller's Attorney
■ Name:	_____	_____
■ Phone numbers:	_____	_____
■ Fax number:	_____	_____
■ E-mail address:	_____	_____

■ ELEMENTS OF THE ONE TO FOUR FAMILY RESIDENTIAL CONTRACT (RESALE)

The Heading

Before we look at the three Ps (parties, property, and price), take a moment to examine the beginning of the form, its title, and its statement of intended use (*see* Figure 3.1). The forms may also carry a notice of purposes for which the form was not designed.

The heading of this form indicates the following:

■ Its intended use (the title)
■ It is for resale, not new construction

- It is only for one to four family properties
- It is not for use with condominiums
- It is promulgated (we must use it)

The date in the upper right corner is the date that TREC approved and promulgated the form. Licensees must be aware of the date and verify they are using the current form. Using an old form is a violation of the TRELA.

FIGURE 3.1

One to Four Family Residential Contract Heading

PROMULGATED BY THE TEXAS REAL ESTATE COMMISSION (TREC)   11-2-2015
ONE TO FOUR FAMILY RESIDENTIAL CONTRACT (RESALE)
NOTICE: Not For Use For Condominium Transactions

Parties

> The promise in Paragraph 1 is known as the consideration in the contract.

Licensees must carefully fill in the names of the parties in paragraph 1 (Parties). If the sellers can provide the listing agent copies of their original documents (Title Policy, Deed, Deed of Trust, etc.) from their purchase, the agent can use those documents to verify proper (legal) names for the seller. The buyers have to provide identification at the time of closing.

Because Texas is a community property state, the licensee will need to furnish marital status. The following are acceptable ways to identify the parties:

- Unmarried
  — NAME, an unmarried person
  — Note: Widows and widowers are unmarried persons
  — Example: Sue Smith, an unmarried person

- Married (When spouse is not joining in the conveyance)
  — NAME, as separate property
  — Example: Steve Swan, as separate property

- Married (Community property)
  — NAME and [husband/wife] NAME
  — Example: Jim Johnson and wife Susan Johnson

- Unmarried persons buying together
  — NAME and NAME, as tenants in common
  — Note: When parties wish to create rights of survivorship or fractional interests are involved, the parties should be advised to seek the advice of a competent real estate attorney before proceeding to prepare an offer to purchase.
  — Example: Sue Smith and John Jones, as tenants in common

- Executor or Administrator of an Estate
  — Executor's or administrator's NAME, executor (administrator) of the estate of (decedent's NAME), deceased
  — Example: Tom Harold, Executor of the estate of Ron Harold, deceased

- General partnership
  - Business NAME, a Texas partnership, or
  - Business NAME, a Texas partnership composed of NAME, NAME, and NAME

- Limited partnership
  - Business NAME, a Texas limited partnership, NAME, as general partner acting for and on behalf of the partnership

- Corporation
  - Company NAME, a Texas* corporation
    *or the name of the state in which the corporation is chartered
  - Note: A corporate resolution, issued by the board of directors, grants the authority to and identifies the officers who can sign on behalf of the corporation. A licensee should request a copy of the corporate resolution prior to the execution of any written agreements. It is to be retained in the transaction file.

- Texas Limited Liability Company
  - Company NAME, a Texas limited liability company
  - Company NAME, LLC

- Nonprofit
  - NAME, NAME, and NAME, trustees for and on behalf of (corporate name)

Property

Paragraph 2A is the legal description, and 2B and 2C describe items to remain with the property unless specifically excluded in 2D.

The property specifics are discussed in paragraph 2 (Property).

Obtaining the correct **legal description** is essential to having a valid contract. The Statute of Frauds requires that any agreement affecting the title to real estate have a valid legal description.

If the property is located within a city, it will probably have a legal description that is part of a recorded plat. For example, Lot 12, Block 15, Greenwich Subdivision, City of Carrollton, County of Dallas. The street address and ZIP code are added for convenience and are required by the TREC form.

If the property is not within a city, use *Unincorporated* or *None* on the form for City.

If the property has a metes-and-bounds legal description, put N/A in the blanks for lot and block, and add an attachment to the contract with the description. The attachment can be made by copying the legal description in the seller's deed or title policy, for example.

The agent must be very aware of all of the items listed in paragraphs 2B Improvements and 2C Accessories. The TAR Listing Agreement uses this same list of items that stay with the property. The listing agent will need to determine if the seller really intends to leave all of these items. Any item that will not remain needs to be listed under paragraph 2D Exclusions. If there are no exclusions, enter

N/A or *None* in the space provided for the purpose of listing any exclusions in paragraph 2D.

It is important to verify that both buyers and sellers carefully read and understand what does and does not stay with the property at closing, because this is no place for assumptions and guesswork. A clear understanding of the form, in addition to fostering realistic expectations, creates the atmosphere for happy buyers and sellers after closing. The best time to address with the sellers which accessories are included or excluded in the sale is at the listing appointment.

Non-Realty Items

If the parties insist upon adding some additional items of personal property (**non-realty items**) that are to stay with the property (that are not already listed in 2B or 2C), attach TREC's Non-Realty Items Addendum to the contract.

- **What needs to be filled out?**   The parties to a sale have agreed that the purchaser will get to keep the free standing bookcase in the living room. The seller is asking the buyer for the nominal fee of $25 to pay for the bookcase and buyer is in agreement. Is this covered under 2B? 2C? If not, how should this situation be handled?
- Answer: A free-standing bookcase is not covered under 2B or 2C. Complete the Non-Realty Items Addendum, being as specific as you can about the bookcase and shelf. Complete paragraph 22 of the One to Four Family Residential Contract (check Other and then put Non-Realty Items Addendum in the blank).

Sales Price

> Paragraph 3A is the down payment, 3B is the total of all loans, and 3C is the sales price.

Paragraph 3 (Sales Price) is one of the easiest to complete correctly. Enter the sales price in 3C.

If this is an all cash offer, 3A and 3C will be the same amount. 3B will be -0-.

If the buyer is obtaining financing for a portion of the sales price, the total of all the financing will be entered in paragraph 3B. Note that 3B excludes any loan funding fee or mortgage insurance premium.

- **Example:**   The buyer is assuming a first lien note with an outstanding balance of $283,400, taking a home improvement loan with a balance of $21,680, and asking the Seller to carry back a note for $80,000. To get the correct number to enter in 3B, add $283,400 + $21,680 + $80,000 for a total of $385,080. To get the correct number to put in 3A, simply subtract 3B from 3C.

Paragraph 3B (Sum of All Financing) gives three different financing possibilities: (1) Third Party Financing, (2) Assumption, and (3) Seller Financing. Each of these requires a different addendum to be attached to the contract.

Third Party Financing   **Third party financing**, paragraph 3B, is any type of new financing that is done by anyone that is a third party (not the seller or the buyer).

If the buyer is obtaining two loans, such as an 80% first lien mortgage and a 20% second lien, the two will be added together for paragraph 3B. Keeping the first lien mortgage at or below 80% saves the buyer the cost of private mortgage insurance.

Assumption Paragraph 3B of the One to Four Family Residential Contract (Sales Price) also provides for the possibility of the buyer's assumption of the seller's existing loan. If that is the case, check Loan Assumption Addendum in 3B and attach the Loan Assumption Addendum.

Seller Financing The final option in paragraph 3B of the One to Four Family Residential Contract is **Seller Financing**. If Seller Financing is being used, either alone or in conjunction with an Assumption or Third Party Financing, check Seller Financing Addendum in 3C and attach the Seller Financing Addendum.

■ THIRD PARTY FINANCING ADDENDUM

The first page of the Third Party Financing Addendum clarifies that the buyer will be applying for the financing promptly and will provide the lender with the documentation needed to make a loan decision.

Paragraphs A1 through A6 describe the third party financing. Notice that A1(b) (Conventional Financing) provides for a second lien, if being used.

The terms described here must be available. For example, it would make no sense to cap the interest rate at 3.5% when nothing is available at less than 4%. Interest is a not-to-exceed figure, so with the buyer's permission, you can allow a little room for change here.

If this is a fixed-rate mortgage, interest will be the same for the entire term of the loan. Therefore, the statement will be "interest not to exceed ___% per annum for the first 30 years of the loan" if the loan has a 30-year term. If it is an adjustable-rate mortgage that will adjust in one year, it will be "per annum for the first one year of the loan." Any adjustment caps or lifetime caps for an adjustable-rate mortgage will need to be described in Special Provisions, paragraph 11 of the contract.

Having the various programs listed here (e.g., Texas Veterans Loan) is a good reminder of the programs that are available. Good agents will learn about each program and ensure they have a lender on their team who can help the buyer with any of them. Buyer's circumstances dictate which program is best for them.

On the second page of the Third Party Financing Addendum, paragraph B describes buyer approval and property approval. Both approvals are needed to have full loan approval.

Paragraph B1 gives the buyers the right to terminate and receive an earnest money refund if the lender says they do not meet the buyer requirements and if it is within the number of days agreed to by the parties. The buyers must terminate within that certain number of days or they will lose their right to terminate under this addendum, and there will no longer be any financing contingency on this contract. If the loan fails after this date because of the buyer, the buyer will be in default.

Paragraph B2 describes the property approval. Notice that property approval can take up to the closing date. It is not limited to the time for buyer approval. If the property does not meet the lender's requirements, the buyer may terminate.

Paragraph B3 states that, "time is of the essence for **this paragraph**." This is one of only six places these words are used in the promulgated forms.

Paragraph C describes the vendor's (seller's) lien that will be on the property. The seller has a lien until the seller is paid in full.

Paragraph D is language required by FHA and VA. They want to ensure that the buyer is not obligated to purchase the property if the appraisal is not enough for the lender to make the loan described here. If the property is not approved by the lender (appraisal, insurability, and lender-required repairs), the buyer has the option to terminate and receive his earnest money back. If the buyer elects to go forward with a smaller loan amount, he will be paying the difference in the cash down payment. Another option is that the seller may be willing to reduce the sales price to the appraised value.

Under new legislation, the lender may require real estate agents to have written authority from the buyer to review the loan documents or closing statement. Paragraph E gives the agent the written authorization.

Loan Programs Listed on the Third Party Financing Addendum

Conventional and Government-Backed Loans   Mortgages can be defined as either government-backed or conventional. Government agencies like the Federal Housing Administration (FHA) and the Department of Veterans Affairs (VA) insure home loans, which are made by private lenders. This insurance is paid for by fees collected from mortgage borrowers. The U.S. Department of Agriculture (USDA) loans money to lower-income borrowers through its Direct Housing Program. It also guarantees loans made by private lenders through its Guaranteed Housing Loans program. This backing is paid for by borrowers. Mortgage loans that are not guaranteed or insured by the government are called conventional loans. Some conventional loans are insured by private mortgage insurance and paid for by borrowers.

Texas Veterans Loans   The State of Texas honors Texas veterans in a very unique way. Funds are set aside to help Texas veterans buy a home at interest rates below the market rates. Even if veterans have used their VA benefit, they might still be able to qualify for this unique program. There are several advantages of a VA loan, including
- lower fixed rates,
- lower closing costs,
- easier approval process,
- lower payments, and
- no mortgage insurance.

FHA Loans   FHA loans are popular with mortgage borrowers because of lower down payment requirements and less stringent lending standards. Simply stated, an FHA loan is a mortgage insured by the Federal Housing Administration, a government agency within the U.S. Department of Housing and Urban Development. Borrowers with FHA loans pay for mortgage insurance, which protects the lender from a loss if the borrower defaults on the loan.

VA Loans   A VA loan is a mortgage loan in the United States guaranteed by the VA. The loan may be issued by qualified lenders. The VA loan was designed to offer long-term financing to eligible American veterans or their surviving spouses (provided they do not remarry).

USDA Loans   Texas USDA mortgage loans, often referred to as Rural Development or RD loans, may be the best choice for a Texas home loan. USDA loans are government-guaranteed home mortgages for borrowers living in rural and suburban communities in Texas.

There are many benefits to Texas USDA loans. In addition to low fixed rates and no mortgage insurance, USDA loans are the only home mortgage available to the general public that will allow borrowers to finance up to 100%. In other words, USDA loans offer no-money-down home loans. Simply put, if you live in a suburban or rural community, you will not find a better home mortgage option.

Reverse Mortgage Financing   A reverse mortgage is special financing for people over the age of 62. Some facts about reverse mortgage purchases include the following:

- They have a very low loan-to-value ratio based on age of the borrower. They require a large down payment. Up-front fees can be large.
- The property must remain owner occupied. Taxes and insurance must be paid.
- There are no monthly payments. Interest is added to the loan balance monthly so the balance increases, rather than decreases, each month.
- The buyer does not have to qualify.
- The owner still owns the property, and it passes to the heirs at the time of the owner's death. The heirs can pay off the mortgage and keep the property or let the lender take it back.
- It is a non-recourse loan, so all the lender gets is the property.
- It may enable a buyer with $100,000 cash to buy a much more expensive home and still have no monthly payments.

L E T ' S   P R A C T I C E   # 1

Sales price: $250,000
80% conventional loan, 30-year fixed rate at 7%
20% cash down payment
Contract will be contingent upon financing
2 discount points, 1% origination fee

Using this information, fill out the following sections of the One to Four Family Residential Contract and the Third Party Financing Addendum, and then check your answers.

One to Four Family Residential Contract

3. SALES PRICE:
A. Cash portion of Sales Price payable by Buyer at closing............................ $_____
B. Sum of all financing described in the attached: ❏   Third Party Financing Addendum,
  ❏   Loan Assumption Addendum, ❏   Seller Financing Addendum .... $_____
C. Sales Price (Sum of A and B)... $_____

Third Party Financing Addendum

❏ 1. <u>Conventional Financing</u>:
  ❏ (a) A first mortgage loan in the principal amount of $ _____ (excluding
    any financed PMI premium), due in full in _____ year(s), with interest not to exceed
    _____% per annum for the first _____ year(s) of the loan with Origination Charges as
    shown on Buyer's Loan Estimate for the loan not to exceed _____% of the loan.
  ❏ (b) A second mortgage loan in the principal amount of $_____(excluding
    any financed PMI premium), due in full in _____year(s), with interest not to exceed
    _____% per annum for the first _____year(s) of the loan with Origination Charges as
    shown on Buyer's Loan Estimate for the loan not to exceed _____% of the loan.

L E T ' S   P R A C T I C E   # 1   A N S W E R S

One to Four Family Residential Contract

3. SALES PRICE:
A. Cash portion of Sales Price payable by Buyer at closing............................ $_____50,000____
B. Sum of all financing described in the attached: ☑   Third Party Financing Addendum,
  ❏   Loan Assumption Addendum, ❏   Seller Financing Addendum .... $_____200,000____
C. Sales Price (Sum of A and B)... $_____250,000____

Third Party Financing Addendum

☑ 1. <u>Conventional Financing</u>:
  ☑ (a) A first mortgage loan in the principal amount of $ _____200,000 (excluding
    any financed PMI premium), due in full in ___30___ year(s), with interest not to exceed
    _7___% per annum for the first ___30___ year(s) of the loan with Origination Charges as
    shown on Buyer's Loan Estimate for the loan not to exceed ____3____% of the loan.
  ❏ (b) A second mortgage loan in the principal amount of $_____(excluding
    any financed PMI premium), due in full in _____year(s), with interest not to exceed
    _____% per annum for the first _____year(s) of the loan with Origination Charges as
    shown on Buyer's Loan Estimate for the loan not to exceed _____% of the loan.

L E T ' S   P R A C T I C E   # 2

Sales price: $185,000
80% conventional first-lien mortgage, 25 years at 6.5% and
10% second lien, 15 years at 8%
10% cash down payment
Contract will be contingent upon financing
0 discount point, 1% origination fee

Using this information, fill out the following sections of the One to Four Family Residential Contract and the Third Party Financing Addendum, and then check your answers.

One to Four Family Residential Contract

3. SALES PRICE:
A. Cash portion of Sales Price payable by Buyer at closing.............................. $_____
B. Sum of all financing described in the attached: ❏   Third Party Financing Addendum,
     ❏   Loan Assumption Addendum, ❏   Seller Financing Addendum .... $_____
C. Sales Price (Sum of A and B).. $_____

Third Party Financing Addendum

❏ 1. Conventional Financing:
  ❏ (a) A first mortgage loan in the principal amount of $ _____ (excluding
     any financed PMI premium), due in full in _____ year(s), with interest not to exceed
     ____% per annum for the first _____ year(s) of the loan with Origination Charges as
     shown on Buyer's Loan Estimate for the loan not to exceed _____% of the loan.
  ❏ (b) A second mortgage loan in the principal amount of $_____(excluding
     any financed PMI premium), due in full in _____year(s), with interest not to exceed
     ____% per annum for the first _____year(s) of the loan with Origination Charges as
     shown on Buyer's Loan Estimate for the loan not to exceed _____% of the loan.

LET'S PRACTICE #2 ANSWERS

One to Four Family Residential Contract

3. SALES PRICE:
A. Cash portion of Sales Price payable by Buyer at closing.............................. $_____18,500
B. Sum of all financing described in the attached: ☑   Third Party Financing Addendum,
     ❏   Loan Assumption Addendum, ❏   Seller Financing Addendum .... $_____166,500
C. Sales Price (Sum of A and B).. $_____185,000

Third Party Financing Addendum

☑ 1. Conventional Financing:
  ☑ (a) A first mortgage loan in the principal amount of $ _____148,000 (excluding
     any financed PMI premium), due in full in ___25___ year(s), with interest not to exceed
     _6.5_% per annum for the first ___25___ year(s) of the loan with Origination Charges as
     shown on Buyer's Loan Estimate for the loan not to exceed ___1___% of the loan.
  ☑ (b) A second mortgage loan in the principal amount of $_____18,500(excluding
     any financed PMI premium), due in full in ___15___year(s), with interest not to exceed
     _8_% per annum for the first ___15___year(s) of the loan with Origination Charges as
     shown on Buyer's Loan Estimate for the loan not to exceed ___0___% of the loan.

LET'S PRACTICE #3

Sales price: $295,000
80% conventional loan, 4.5% ARM, adjustable after one year
20% cash down payment, 30-year loan
Contract will be contingent upon financing
1 discount point, 1% origination fee

Using this information, fill out the following sections of the One to Four Family Residential Contract and the Third Party Financing Addendum, and then check your answers.

One to Four Family Residential Contract

3. SALES PRICE:
A. Cash portion of Sales Price payable by Buyer at closing.............................. $_____
B. Sum of all financing described in the attached: ❏   Third Party Financing Addendum,
     ❏   Loan Assumption Addendum, ❏   Seller Financing Addendum .... $_____
C. Sales Price (Sum of A and B).. $_____

Third Party Financing Addendum

☐ 1. <u>Conventional Financing</u>:

    ☐ (a) A first mortgage loan in the principal amount of $ _____ (excluding any financed PMI premium), due in full in _____ year(s), with interest not to exceed _____% per annum for the first _____ year(s) of the loan with Origination Charges as shown on Buyer's Loan Estimate for the loan not to exceed _____% of the loan.

    ☐ (b) A second mortgage loan in the principal amount of $_____ (excluding any financed PMI premium), due in full in _____year(s), with interest not to exceed _____% per annum for the first _____year(s) of the loan with Origination Charges as shown on Buyer's Loan Estimate for the loan not to exceed _____% of the loan.

LET'S PRACTICE #3 ANSWERS

One to Four Family Residential Contract

3. SALES PRICE:

A. Cash portion of Sales Price payable by Buyer at closing .... $_____ 59,000

B. Sum of all financing described in the attached: ☑ Third Party Financing Addendum,
    ☐ Loan Assumption Addendum, ☐ Seller Financing Addendum .... $_____ 236,000

C. Sales Price (Sum of A and B) .... $_____ 295,000

Third Party Financing Addendum for Credit Approval

☑ 1. <u>Conventional Financing</u>:

    ☑ (a) A first mortgage loan in the principal amount of $ _____ 236,000 (excluding any financed PMI premium), due in full in ___30___ year(s), with interest not to exceed __4.5__% per annum for the first ___1___ year(s) of the loan with Origination Charges as shown on Buyer's Loan Estimate for the loan not to exceed ___2___% of the loan.

    ☐ (b) A second mortgage loan in the principal amount of $_____(excluding any financed PMI premium), due in full in _____year(s), with interest not to exceed _____% per annum for the first _____year(s) of the loan with Origination Charges as shown on Buyer's Loan Estimate for the loan not to exceed _____% of the loan.

■ LOAN ASSUMPTION ADDENDUM

If the buyer is going to assume the seller's existing loan, check Loan Assumption Addendum in paragraph 3B on the One to Four Family Residential Contract and attach the Loan Assumption Addendum.

Paragraph A of the Loan Assumption Addendum (Credit Documentation) gives the parties the opportunity to negotiate for the buyer to provide the seller with items to establish creditworthiness. The items must be delivered to the seller within the time negotiated in the blank.

Paragraph B (Credit Approval) starts off by giving the seller the right to terminate if the items are not received within the time frame. If the seller is going to terminate, the seller must do so within seven days after expiration of the time for delivery and give notice to the buyer. In this case, the seller receives the earnest money.

The seller also has the right to terminate if the items are received within the time frame, but the seller determines that the buyer's credit is not acceptable. The seller must terminate within seven days after expiration of the time for delivery. In this event, the buyer receives the earnest money.

If the seller does not terminate within these seven-day periods, the seller loses the right to terminate and is deemed to have approved the buyer's creditworthiness.

Paragraph C of the Loan Assumption Addendum (Assumption) describes the note(s) that is/are being assumed and cautions the buyer that the obligations imposed by the deed of trust securing these notes will continue.

Paragraph C(1) describes any first lien note being assumed, and paragraph C(2) describes any second lien note being assumed. Because the payments on an assumed loan are already set up, the buyer will follow the same payment schedule, starting with the first payment after the closing. For example, if the seller has paid the January 1 and February 1 payments and then the loans are assumed on February 15, the buyer's first payment will be March 1.

The paragraph at the bottom of this section addresses two things:

1. It discusses what will happen if the balance varies. Because the cash + the loan balance = the sales price, if the loan balance varies, either the cash or the sales price must be adjusted. The parties check the appropriate box to make that choice.
2. It gives either party the right to terminate if the variance exceeds $500, unless the other party elects to pay the excess. If the parties terminate the contract for this reason, the earnest money will be refunded to buyer.

Paragraphs D and E of the Loan Assumption Addendum (Loan Assumption Terms and Consent by Noteholder) protect the buyer in the event the lender should charge an assumption fee or an interest rate more than what was agreed to or refuses to consent to the assumption. In any of these events, the earnest money will be refunded to the buyer.

Paragraph F of the Loan Assumption Addendum states, "SELLER'S LIENS. Unless seller is released from liability on any assumed note, a vendor's lien and deed of trust to secure assumption will be required. The vendor's lien will automatically be released on delivery of an executed release by noteholder." This protects the seller in the event the lender does not release the seller from liability. The seller would have a lien on the property and the ability to pay any delinquency to get the property back. The vendor's (seller's) lien is released when the lender relieves the seller of future liability.

Paragraph G of the Loan Assumption Addendum states, "TAX AND INSURANCE ESCROW. If noteholder maintains an escrow account for ad valorem taxes, casualty insurance premiums or mortgage insurance premiums, Seller shall transfer the escrow account to Buyer without any deficiency. Buyer shall reimburse Seller for the amount in the transferred accounts." This protects both parties. If there is a deficiency in the tax and insurance escrow account, the seller has to pay the deficiency. The buyer reimburses the seller for the amount in the account, so if there is any overage in the account, the seller is paid for it.

In the notices and signatures section of the Loan Assumption Addendum, both the buyer and the seller need to read and pay attention to the important information in the notices. These are things that sometimes the parties do not understand, and it is critical information.

LET'S PRACTICE #4

Sales price: $185,000
Buyer is going to assume seller's existing mortgage with ABC Lenders. The principal balance of the loan is $123,655. The seller's current monthly payments are $875.91. If the balance varies at closing, the parties agree to adjust the cash down payment. The 30-year loan has a 5.5% fixed rate and is assumable at the current rate. The lender says the assumption fee will be 1% of the loan amount.

Using this information, fill out the following sections of the One to Four Family Residential Contract and the Loan Assumption Addendum, and then check your answers.

One to Four Family Residential Contract

3. SALES PRICE:
  A. Cash portion of Sales Price payable by Buyer at closing.............................. $_____
  B. Sum of all financing described in the attached: ❑ Third Party Financing Addendum,
     ❑ Loan Assumption Addendum, ❑ Seller Financing Addendum .... $_____
  C. Sales Price (Sum of A and B).. $_____

Loan Assumption Addendum

  C. ASSUMPTION.   Buyer's assumption of an existing note includes all obligations imposed by the deed of trust securing the note.
    ❑ (1) The unpaid principal balance of a first lien promissory note payable to_____
       _____which unpaid balance at closing will be $ _____.
       The total current monthly payment including principal, interest and any reserve deposits is $ _____. Buyer's initial payment will be the first payment due after closing.

    ❑ (2) The unpaid principal balance of a second lien promissory note payable to _____
       _____which unpaid balance at closing will be $ _____.
       The total current monthly payment including principal, interest and any reserve deposits is $ _____. Buyer's initial payment will be the first payment due after closing.

    If the unpaid principal balance of any assumed loan as of the Closing Date varies from the loan balance stated above, the ❑ cash payable at closing ❑ Sales Price will be adjusted by the amount of any variance. If the total principal balance of all assumed loans varies in an amount greater than $500 at closing, either party may terminate this contract and the earnest money will be refunded to Buyer unless the other party elects to pay the excess of the variance.

  D. LOAN ASSUMPTION TERMS.   Buyer may terminate this contract and the earnest money will be refunded to Buyer if the noteholder requires:
    (1) payment of an assumption fee in excess of $ _____in C(1) or $ _____in C(2) and Seller declines to pay such excess, or
    (2) an increase in the interest rate to more than _____% in C(1) or_____% in C(2), or
    (3) any other modification of the loan documents.

LET'S PRACTICE #4 ANSWERS

One to Four Family Residential Contract

3. SALES PRICE:
  A. Cash portion of Sales Price payable by Buyer at closing.............................. $_____ 61,345
  B. Sum of all financing described in the attached: ❑ Third Party Financing Addendum,
     ☑ Loan Assumption Addendum, ❑ Seller Financing Addendum .... $_____ 123,655
  C. Sales Price (Sum of A and B).. $_____ 185,000

Loan Assumption Addendum

C. ASSUMPTION. Buyer's assumption of an existing note includes all obligations imposed by the deed of trust securing the note.
☑ (1) The unpaid principal balance of a first lien promissory note payable to <u>ABC Lenders</u>
_____ which unpaid balance at closing will be $ _____<u>123,655</u>.
The total current monthly payment including principal, interest and any reserve deposits is
$ _____<u>875.91</u>. Buyer's initial payment will be the first payment due after closing.

☐ (2) The unpaid principal balance of a second lien promissory note payable to _____
_____ which unpaid balance at closing will be $ _____.
The total current monthly payment including principal, interest and any reserve deposits is
$ _____. Buyer's initial payment will be the first payment due after closing.

If the unpaid principal balance of any assumed loan as of the Closing Date varies from the loan balance stated above, the ☑ cash payable at closing ☐ Sales Price will be adjusted by the amount of any variance. If the total principal balance of all assumed loans varies in an amount greater than $500 at closing, either party may terminate this contract and the earnest money will be refunded to Buyer unless the other party elects to pay the excess of the variance.

D. LOAN ASSUMPTION TERMS. Buyer may terminate this contract and the earnest money will be refunded to Buyer if the noteholder requires:
(1) payment of an assumption fee in excess of $ ____<u>1,236.55</u> in C(1) or $ _____<u>NA</u> in C(2) and Seller declines to pay such excess, or
(2) an increase in the interest rate to more than __<u>5.5</u>__% in C(1) or <u>NA</u>% in C(2), or
(3) any other modification of the loan documents.

■ SELLER FINANCING ADDENDUM

If Seller Financing is being used, either alone or in conjunction with an Assumption or Third Party Financing, check Seller Financing Addendum in paragraph 3B in the One to Four Family Residential Contract and attach the Seller Financing Addendum.

The first few paragraphs of the Seller Financing Addendum are like those in the Loan Assumption Addendum. Paragraph A of the Seller Financing Addendum gives the parties the opportunity to negotiate for the buyer to provide the seller with items to establish creditworthiness. The items must be delivered to the seller within the time negotiated in the blank.

Paragraph B starts off by giving the seller the right to terminate if the items are not received within the time frame. If the seller is going to terminate, the seller must do so within seven days after expiration of the time for delivery and give notice to the buyer. In this case, the seller receives the earnest money.

The seller also has the right to terminate if the items are received within the time frame, but the seller determines that the buyer's credit is not acceptable. The seller must terminate within seven days after expiration of the time for delivery. In this event, the buyer receives the earnest money.

If the seller does not terminate within these seven day periods, the seller loses the right to terminate and is deemed to have approved the buyer's creditworthiness.

Paragraph C of the Seller Financing Addendum describes the amount of the promissory note, the rate of interest for the loan, the buyer's right of prepayment of the loan, and the seller's right to collect late charges if payments are not received on time. It also provides the parties with three choices for loan repayment.

Paragraph D(1) of the Seller Financing Addendum discusses what will happen if the property is sold. Most sellers will want the right to give their consent to any sale of the property while they still have an outstanding loan secured by the property. D(1)(b) describes the seller's right to declare the balance of the loan due if the property is sold without consent.

The note under D(1)(b) reminds buyers that their liability continues until the loan is paid in full unless they receive a release of liability from the seller.

Paragraph D(2) of the Seller Financing Addendum gives the parties an option to negotiate a requirement for a tax and insurance escrow account. Because seller financing can be used in many situations and in conjunction with other financing, many times there is not a need for an escrow account. For example, if a buyer is assuming a seller's first lien mortgage, with XYZ Savings and the seller financing is a second lien, only for a portion of the seller's equity, XYZ Savings might already be collecting a monthly escrow payment.

The same situation may exist if the buyer is getting new financing and the first lien mortgage company is carrying an escrow account. For example, on an 80/10/10, the first lien company may have an 80% loan and the seller may have a 10% loan. In this case, there may be no need for the seller to carry an escrow account because the first lien mortgage company is doing so.

If the seller financing is the only loan, and the seller wants to make sure the money will be there to pay the taxes and insurance when they are due, the seller may require a monthly amount to cover payments of those items.

Paragraph D(3) protects the seller by making a default on any superior lien a default under the seller's lien.

LET'S PRACTICE #5

Sales price: $325,000
80%, 15-year, new conventional loan, 6% fixed rate
10% cash down payment
10% seller financing for 120 payments, no escrow required,
7% fixed rate, $543.12 monthly, including interest,
consent required for transfer
Contract will be contingent upon financing
1 discount point, 1% origination fee

Using this information, fill out the following sections of the One to Four Family Residential Contract, Third Party Financing Addendum, and Seller Financing Addendum, and then check your answers.

One to Four Family Residential Contract

3. SALES PRICE:
   A. Cash portion of Sales Price payable by Buyer at closing .... $_____
   B. Sum of all financing described in the attached: ❏ Third Party Financing Addendum,
      ❏ Loan Assumption Addendum, ❏ Seller Financing Addendum .... $_____
   C. Sales Price (Sum of A and B)... $_____

Third Party Financing Addendum

❑ 1. <u>Conventional Financing</u>:

    ❑ (a) A first mortgage loan in the principal amount of $ _____ (excluding any financed PMI premium), due in full in _____ year(s), with interest not to exceed _____% per annum for the first _____ year(s) of the loan with Origination Charges as shown on Buyer's Loan Estimate for the loan not to exceed _____% of the loan.

    ❑ (b) A second mortgage loan in the principal amount of $_____ (excluding any financed PMI premium), due in full in _____ year(s), with interest not to exceed _____% per annum for the first _____ year(s) of the loan with Origination Charges as shown on Buyer's Loan Estimate for the loan not to exceed _____% of the loan.

Seller Financing Addendum

C. PROMISSORY NOTE. The promissory note in the amount of $_____(Note), included in Paragraph 3B of the contract payable by Buyer to the order of Seller will bear interest at the rate of _____% per annum and be payable at the place designated by Seller. Buyer may prepay the Note in whole or in part at any time without penalty. Any prepayments are to be applied to the payment of the installments of principal last maturing and interest will immediately cease on the prepaid principal. The Note will contain a provision for payment of a late fee of 5% of any installment not paid within 10 days of the due date. Matured unpaid amounts will bear interest at the rate of 1½% per month or at the highest lawful rate, whichever is less. The Note will be payable as follows:

    ❑ (1) In one payment due _____ after the date of the Note with interest payable ❑ at maturity ❑ monthly ❑ quarterly. (check one box only)

    ❑ (2) In monthly installments of $ _____ ❑ including interest ❑plus interest (check one box only) beginning _____ after the date of the Note and continuing monthly thereafter for_____ months when the balance of the Note will be due and payable.

    ❑ (3) Interest only in monthly installments for the first _____ month(s) and thereafter in installments of $_____ ❑ including interest ❑ plus interest (check one box only) beginning _____ after the date of the Note and continuing monthly thereafter for_____ months when the balance of the Note will be due and payable.

D. DEED OF TRUST. The deed of trust securing the Note will provide for the following:

  (1) PROPERTY TRANSFERS: (check one box only)

    ❑ (a) Consent Not Required: The Property may be sold, conveyed or leased without the consent of Seller, provided any subsequent buyer assumes the Note.

    ❑ (b) Consent Required: If all or any part of the Property is sold, conveyed, leased for a period longer than 3 years, leased with an option to purchase, or otherwise sold (including any contract for deed), without Seller's prior written consent, which consent may be withheld in Seller's sole discretion. Seller may declare the balance of the Note to be immediately due and payable. The creation of a subordinate lien, any conveyance under threat or order of condemnation, any deed solely between buyers, or the passage of title by reason of the death of a buyer or by operation of law will not entitle Seller to exercise the remedies provided in this paragraph.

    NOTE: *Under (a) or (b), Buyer's liability to pay the Note will continue unless Buyer obtains a release of liability from Seller.*

  (2) TAX AND INSURANCE ESCROW: (check one box only)

    ❑ (a) Escrow Not Required: Buyer shall furnish Seller, before each year's ad valorem taxes become delinquent, evidence that all ad valorem taxes on the Property have been paid. Buyer shall annually furnish Seller evidence of paid-up casualty insurance naming Seller as a mortgagee loss payee.

    ❑ (b) Escrow Required: With each installment Buyer shall deposit in escrow with Seller a pro rata part of the estimated annual ad valorem taxes and casualty insurance premiums for the Property. Buyer shall pay any deficiency within 30 days after notice from Seller. Buyer's failure to pay the deficiency will be a default under the deed of trust. Buyer is not required to deposit any escrow payments for taxes and insurance that are deposited with a superior lienholder. The casualty insurance must name Seller as a mortgagee loss payee.

  (3) PRIOR LIENS: Any default under any lien superior to the lien securing the Note will be a default under the deed of trust securing the Note.

LET'S PRACTICE #5 ANSWERS

One to Four Family Residential Contract

3. SALES PRICE:
A. Cash portion of Sales Price payable by Buyer at closing .... $ _____32,500_____
B. Sum of all financing described in the attached: ☑ Third Party Financing Addendum,
     ❏ Loan Assumption Addendum, ☑ Seller Financing Addendum .... $ _____292,500_____
C. Sales Price (Sum of A and B) .... $ _____325,000_____

Third Party Financing Addendum

☑ 1. <u>Conventional Financing</u>:
    ☑ (a) A first mortgage loan in the principal amount of $ _____260,000_____ (excluding any financed PMI premium), due in full in ___15___ year(s), with interest not to exceed __6__% per annum for the first ___15___ year(s) of the loan with Origination Charges as shown on Buyer's Loan Estimate for the loan not to exceed ___2___ % of the loan.
    ❏ (b) A second mortgage loan in the principal amount of $_____(excluding any financed PMI premium), due in full in _____year(s), with interest not to exceed _____% per annum for the first _____year(s) of the loan with Origination Charges as shown on Buyer's Loan Estimate for the loan not to exceed _____% of the loan.

Seller Financing Addendum

C. PROMISSORY NOTE. The promissory note in the amount of $_____32,500_(Note), included in Paragraph 3B of the contract payable by Buyer to the order of Seller will bear interest at the rate of __7__% per annum and be payable at the place designated by Seller. Buyer may prepay the Note in whole or in part at any time without penalty. Any prepayments are to be applied to the payment of the installments of principal last maturing and interest will immediately cease on the prepaid principal. The Note will contain a provision for payment of a late fee of 5% of any installment not paid within 10 days of the due date. Matured unpaid amounts will bear interest at the rate of 1½% per month or at the highest lawful rate, whichever is less. The Note will be payable as follows:

    ❏ (1) In one payment due _____ after the date of the Note with interest payable ❏ at maturity ❏ monthly ❏ quarterly. (check one box only)

    ☑ (2) In monthly installments of $ _____543.12_ ☑ including interest ❏plus interest (check one box only) beginning ____the first of the month____ after the date of the Note and continuing monthly thereafter for_____120_____ months when the balance of the Note will be due and payable.

    ❏ (3) Interest only in monthly installments for the first _____ month(s) and thereafter in installments of $_____ ❏ including interest ❏ plus interest (check one box only) beginning _____ after the date of the Note and continuing monthly thereafter for_____ months when the balance of the Note will be due and payable.

D. DEED OF TRUST. The deed of trust securing the Note will provide for the following:

(1) PROPERTY TRANSFERS: (check one box only)

    ❏ (a) Consent Not Required: The Property may be sold, conveyed or leased without the consent of Seller, provided any subsequent buyer assumes the Note.

    ☑ (b) Consent Required: If all or any part of the Property is sold, conveyed, leased for a period longer than 3 years, leased with an option to purchase, or otherwise sold (including any contract for deed), without Seller's prior written consent, which consent may be withheld in Seller's sole discretion, Seller may declare the balance of the Note to be immediately due and payable. The creation of a subordinate lien, any conveyance under threat or order of condemnation, any deed solely between buyers, or the passage of title by reason of the death of a buyer or by operation of law will not entitle Seller to exercise the remedies provided in this paragraph.

    NOTE: *Under (a) or (b), Buyer's liability to pay the Note will continue unless Buyer obtains a release of liability from Seller.*

(2) TAX AND INSURANCE ESCROW: (check one box only)

    ☑ (a) Escrow Not Required: Buyer shall furnish Seller, before each year's ad valorem taxes become delinquent, evidence that all ad valorem taxes on the Property have been paid. Buyer shall annually furnish Seller evidence of paid-up casualty insurance naming Seller as a mortgagee loss payee.

    ❏ (b) Escrow Required: With each installment Buyer shall deposit in escrow with Seller a pro rata part of the estimated annual ad valorem taxes and casualty insurance premiums for the Property. Buyer shall pay any deficiency within 30 days after notice from Seller. Buyer's failure to pay the deficiency will be a default under the deed of trust. Buyer is not required to deposit any escrow payments for taxes and insurance that are deposited with a superior lienholder. The casualty insurance must name Seller as a mortgagee loss payee.

■ ADDENDUM FOR RELEASE OF LIABILITY ON ASSUMED LOAN AND/OR RESTORATION OF SELLER'S VA ENTITLEMENT

As discussed in Chapter 3, assumption of existing financing requires the use of the Loan Assumption Addendum. If, as a condition of permitting assumption of existing financing, the seller wants to make the assumption subject to the seller being released from future liability for the loan, the parties will need to use the Addendum for Release of Liability on Assumed Loan and/or Restoration of Seller's VA Entitlement.

L E T ' S   P R A C T I C E   # 6

Barbara and Ken Johnson are interested in assuming a VA loan on a property they are buying from Mac Smith, a veteran. The unpaid balance on the loan is $125,000 and Mr. Smith is asking $145,000 for the property. The Johnsons have the additional $20,000 to put down. The principal and interest payments on the loan are $925 a month with a 5% interest rate. The loan will be paid off in 20 years. The loan company is Wells Fargo and the parties agree that the buyer will make application to assume the loan within 3 days. Mr. Smith would like to be released from liability on the loan and is not willing to close unless that can happen. He would also like to have his VA benefits restored but is willing to close even if that does not happen. Since the Johnsons are making application with Wells Fargo to assume the loan, Mr. Smith is not asking for any other credit information. The assumption fee will be 1% of the loan balance, and if the balance varies slightly, the parties would like the sales price to be adjusted.

Using this information, fill out the following sections of the One to Four Family Residential Contract, Loan Assumption Addendum, and the Addendum for Release of Liability on Assumed Loan and/or Restoration of Seller's VA Entitlement.

One to Four Family Residential Contract

3. SALES PRICE:
A. Cash portion of Sales Price payable by Buyer at closing.............................. $_____
B. Sum of all financing described in the attached: ❑   Third Party Financing Addendum,
    ❑   Loan Assumption Addendum, ❑   Seller Financing Addendum .... $_____
C. Sales Price (Sum of A and B).. $_____

Loan Assumption Addendum

C. ASSUMPTION.   Buyer's assumption of an existing note includes all obligations imposed by the deed of trust securing the note.
❑ (1) The unpaid principal balance of a first lien promissory note payable to_____
_____which unpaid balance at closing will be $ _____.
The total current monthly payment including principal, interest and any reserve deposits is $ _____. Buyer's initial payment will be the first payment due after closing.

❑ (2) The unpaid principal balance of a second lien promissory note payable to _____
_____which unpaid balance at closing will be $ _____.
The total current monthly payment including principal, interest and any reserve deposits is $ _____. Buyer's initial payment will be the first payment due after closing.

If the unpaid principal balance of any assumed loan as of the Closing Date varies from the loan balance stated above, the ❑ cash payable at closing ❑ Sales Price will be adjusted by the amount of any variance. If the total principal balance of all assumed loans varies in an amount greater than $500 at closing, either party may terminate this contract and the earnest money will be refunded to Buyer unless the other party elects to pay the excess of the variance.

D. LOAN ASSUMPTION TERMS.   Buyer may terminate this contract and the earnest money will be refunded to Buyer if the noteholder requires:
(1) payment of an assumption fee in excess of $ _____in C(1) or $ _____in C(2) and Seller declines to pay such excess, or
(2) an increase in the interest rate to more than _____% in C(1) or_____% in C(2), or
(3) any other modification of the loan documents.

Addendum for Release of Liability on Assumed Loan and/or Restoration of Seller's VA Entitlement

❑ **A. RELEASE OF SELLER'S LIABILITY ON LOAN TO BE ASSUMED:**

Within _____ days after the effective date of this contract Seller and Buyer shall apply for release of Seller's liability from (a) any conventional lender, (b) VA and any lender whose loan has been guaranteed by VA, or (c) FHA and any lender whose loan has been insured by FHA. Seller and Buyer shall furnish all required information and documents. If any release of liability has not been approved by the Closing Date: (check one box only)

❑ (1) This contract will terminate and the earnest money will be refunded to Buyer.

❑ (2) Failure to obtain release approval will not delay closing.

❑ **B. RESTORATION OF SELLER'S ENTITLEMENT FOR VA LOAN:**

Within _____ days after the effective date of this contract Seller and Buyer shall apply for restoration of Seller's VA entitlement and shall furnish all information and documents required by VA. If restoration has not been approved by the Closing Date: (check one box only)

❑ (1) This contract will terminate and the earnest money will be refunded to Buyer.

❑ (2) Failure to obtain restoration approval will not delay closing.

LET'S PRACTICE #6 ANSWERS

One to Four Family Residential Contract

3. SALES PRICE:
A. Cash portion of Sales Price payable by Buyer at closing.............................. $_____ 20,000
B. Sum of all financing described in the attached: ❑ Third Party Financing Addendum,
☑ Loan Assumption Addendum, ❑ Seller Financing Addendum .... $_____ 125,000
C. Sales Price (Sum of A and B).. $_____ 145,000

Loan Assumption Addendum

C. ASSUMPTION. Buyer's assumption of an existing note includes all obligations imposed by the deed of trust securing the note.
☒ (1) The unpaid principal balance of a first lien promissory note payable to Wells Fargo _____ _____which unpaid balance at closing will be $ 125,000 _____. The total current monthly payment including principal, interest and any reserve deposits is $ 925 _____. Buyer's initial payment will be the first payment due after closing.

❑ (2) The unpaid principal balance of a second lien promissory note payable to _____ _____which unpaid balance at closing will be $ _____. The total current monthly payment including principal, interest and any reserve deposits is $ _____. Buyer's initial payment will be the first payment due after closing.

If the unpaid principal balance of any assumed loan as of the Closing Date varies from the loan balance stated above, the ❑ cash payable at closing ☒ Sales Price will be adjusted by the amount of any variance. If the total principal balance of all assumed loans varies in an amount greater than $500 at closing, either party may terminate this contract and the earnest money will be refunded to Buyer unless the other party elects to pay the excess of the variance.

D. LOAN ASSUMPTION TERMS. Buyer may terminate this contract and the earnest money will be refunded to Buyer if the noteholder requires:
(1) payment of an assumption fee in excess of $ 1,250 ___ in C(1) or $ _____in C(2) and Seller declines to pay such excess, or
(2) an increase in the interest rate to more than __5__ % in C(1) or_____% in C(2), or
(3) any other modification of the loan documents.

Addendum for Release of Liability on Assumed Loan and/or Restoration of Seller's VA Entitlement

☒ **A. RELEASE OF SELLER'S LIABILITY ON LOAN TO BE ASSUMED:**

Within ___3___ days after the effective date of this contract Seller and Buyer shall apply for release of Seller's liability from (a) any conventional lender, (b) VA and any lender whose loan has been guaranteed by VA, or (c) FHA and any lender whose loan has been insured by FHA. Seller and Buyer shall furnish all required information and documents. If any release of liability has not been approved by the Closing Date: (check one box only)

☒ (1) This contract will terminate and the earnest money will be refunded to Buyer.

❑ (2) Failure to obtain release approval will not delay closing.

☒ **B. RESTORATION OF SELLER'S ENTITLEMENT FOR VA LOAN:**

Within ___3___ days after the effective date of this contract Seller and Buyer shall apply for restoration of Seller's VA entitlement and shall furnish all information and documents required by VA. If restoration has not been approved by the Closing Date: (check one box only)

❑ (1) This contract will terminate and the earnest money will be refunded to Buyer.

☒ (2) Failure to obtain restoration approval will not delay closing.

SUMMARY

Paragraphs 1 through 3 of the TREC One to Four Family Residential Contract cover the details of the transaction for the parties, the property description, the sales price, and the financing.

Three types of financing are discussed in paragraph 3 (third party, assumption, and seller financing). Each type of financing requires a special addendum to verify the details.

CONTRACT WORKSHOP

1. In an assumption purchase, the buyer was to furnish the seller with credit information by September 25. The seller did not receive it. Can the seller terminate the contract on September 28 if he elects to do so? On October 3?

CHAPTER 3 QUIZ

1. When property owned by a married couple is being sold, what is the *BEST* way to identify the sellers?
   a. Mr. and Mrs. Thomas Bud Smith
   b. Thomas Bud Smith and spouse Mary Ann Smith
   c. Thomas Bud Smith and his wife
   d. Thomas Bud Smith et vir Mary Ann Smith

2. If the Third Party Financing Addendum says credit approval must be obtained within ten days after the effective date, and the appraisal comes in too low for the lender to make the loan on the 12th day, what is the status of the contract?
   a. The buyer is in default.
   b. The contract will terminate, and earnest money and any option money will be refunded to the buyer.
   c. The buyer may terminate the contract, and earnest money will be refunded to seller.
   d. The buyer may terminate the contract, and earnest money will be refunded to buyer.

3. The date in the upper right corner of the promulgated contract form is the date
   a. the Broker-Lawyer Committee drafted the form.
   b. TREC approved and promulgated the form.
   c. licensees must begin using the form.
   d. the form will be reviewed in the future.

4. If the buyer wants to be sure the fireplace screen stays with the property, the buyer's agent should
   a. write it in paragraph 11.
   b. add it the Non-Realty Items Addendum.
   c. add it at the end of paragraph 2.
   d. do nothing; it is already in the contract.

5. If the seller is doing all of the financing and is furnishing the buyer with an owner's policy of title insurance, who will pay for a mortgagee policy of title insurance and who does it protect?
   a. The buyer will pay, and it protects the third-party lender.
   b. The seller will pay, and it protects the third-party lender.
   c. The buyer will pay, and it protects the seller.
   d. The seller will pay, and it protects the buyer.

6. According to the Third Party Financing Addendum, which one of the following is *NOT* necessary for buyer approval?
   a. The terms of the loan described must be available.
   b. An appraisal for at least the sales amount must be received.
   c. The buyer's assets and income meet the lenders underwriting requirements.
   d. The buyer's credit history meets the lender's underwriting requirements.

7. According to the Loan Assumption Addendum, if the buyer does not deliver the credit information within the required time, the seller has how many days to terminate after expiration for the time of delivery?
   a. 10
   b. 3
   c. 5
   d. 7

8. According to the Seller's Financing Addendum, if the buyer delivers his credit information to the seller timely and the seller determines it is unacceptable, how many days after the date for the expiration of the time for delivery does the seller have to terminate?
   a. 7
   b. 3
   c. 5
   d. 12

9. Property approval, according to paragraph B2 in the Third Party Financing Addendum, includes

   a. the appraisal.
   b. lender-required repairs.
   c. insurability.
   d. all of these.

10. In paragraph 3 of the One to Four Family Residential Contract, the sales price is the sum of the cash portion of the sales price

   a. plus all the closing cost.
   b. plus loan funding.
   c. and the sum of all financing.
   d. plus the mortgage insurance premium.

CHAPTER 4

Covenants, Commitments, and Notices

■ **LEARNING OBJECTIVES**   *When you have completed this chapter, you will be able to*

- ■ **identify** the provisions within paragraphs 4 (License Holder Disclosure) and 5 (Earnest Money) of the One to Four Family Residential Contract;
- ■ **identify** the provisions within paragraph 6 (Title Policy and Survey) of the One to Four Family Residential Contract, including notices 1–10; and
- ■ **identify** the provisions within paragraph 7 (Property Condition) of the One to Four Family Residential Contract.

■ KEY TERMS

commitment	license holder disclosure	seller disclosure
earnest money	property condition	survey
escrow	restrictive covenants	title policy
lead paint disclosure		

■ LICENSE HOLDER DISCLOSURE

Paragraph 4 provides a place for disclosure if the real estate license holder is a party to the transaction; if the real estate license holder is acting on behalf of a spouse, parent, child, or business entity in which the license holder owns more than 10%; or if the real estate license holder is a trustee for a trust where the beneficiary is the license holder's spouse, parent, or child.

■ EARNEST MONEY

Paragraph 5 (Earnest Money): Money is placed in escrow as an accessible remedy in case of default; it is NOT consideration of the contract. It is applied to the sales price at funding.

Paragraph 5 of the promulgated contract addresses **earnest money**. Note that earnest money is not necessary to bind the contract. The promise of the purchaser to buy and the promise of the seller to deliver title are adequate consideration to create a legally binding executory contract.

Earnest money serves as liquidated damages in the event of default, as addressed in the identified remedies listed in paragraph 15. It is customary for buyers to offer earnest money, and it has come to be expected by many sellers. It is perceived to indicate a buyer's serious intent to carry out the terms of the contract in good faith. In some cases, it might make an offer more attractive to a seller (e.g., if offers are otherwise identical, but one buyer offers no earnest money and another offers 3% of the purchase price, the seller might be more enticed by the offer with earnest money). It is important to remember that earnest money is not required. Ultimately, it is up to the buyer and seller to decide the proper amount of earnest money for their transaction.

The blanks calling for additional earnest money can be used when the buyer is unable to make the full desired deposit at the time of signing the agreement. For instance, this might occur when the buyer is waiting for a certificate of deposit (CD) to mature. The buyer does not want to delay signing the agreement, but they do not want to cash in the CD early and lose the interest. It should be noted that failure to deposit the earnest money in a timely manner constitutes a default and gives the seller the right to exercise the default remedies established by agreement of the parties in paragraph 15.

TREC rule 535.146 (Maintaining Trust Money) addresses proper handling of earnest money by licensees.

■ OPTION MONEY

An important notice to the seller is in paragraph 23 of the contract. Paragraph 23 of the One to Four Family Residential Contract provides a place for the buyer to pay the seller a sum of money (the option fee) and the seller to grant the buyer a number of negotiated days with the unrestricted right to terminate to contract. According to the contract, the money must be paid to the seller within 3 days. Time is of the essence for this paragraph, so the 3 days is critical. If the option money is not paid within the 3 days the contract is still valid, but paragraph 23 does not exist as part of the contract, therefore the buyer has no right to terminate.

The intent of the option period is to allow the buyer to do their due diligence. Inspections, ability to obtain insurance, and anything else they need to verify should take place within the negotiated option days.

The number of days within which the buyer can terminate is also a critical date. If the date is missed the buyer loses this right to terminate.

The termination option will be discussed further in Chapter 5.

■ TITLE POLICY AND SURVEY

Title Policy

The contract is an agreement between the buyer and the seller and should reflect their wishes. Usually, the company selected to issue the owner's **title policy** in paragraph 6A is the same chosen in paragraph 5 to serve as escrow agent; however, it is not mandatory.

Who should choose the title company? Many would argue that because the seller often pays for the title policy, the seller should choose the company that will issue the policy.

> Paragraph 6: Pay close attention to the performance time frames of the parties.

Who pays does not and should not automatically dictate who chooses something in a real estate transaction. For example, the buyer is usually required to pay for an appraisal when the buyer is seeking a new loan, but it is the lender who selects the appraiser and is the client of the appraiser. When using a loan guaranteed by the Department of Veterans Affairs, the government regulations require that the seller pay the legal fees for the preparation of the note and mortgage instrument for the borrower's loan. Before a seller or listing agent attempts to dictate the title company, it should be noted that the owner's title policy is a contract between the buyer and the title company. Also, a review of the Real Estate Settlement Procedures Act (RESPA), covering one-to four-family residential transactions that have financing related to the federal government, reveals that federal regulation prohibits the seller from requiring the buyer to use the services of a particular title provider. Why should the seller really care? Providing the title policy is an economical way for the seller to show evidence of clear title and indemnify the buyer from financial loss in the event of title failure. For properties with the same sales price, the premium cost to insure the title of the property is the same at all title companies in the state.

The majority of transactions closed in Texas involve the issuance of a title policy to the buyer of the property. Local custom often calls for the owner's policy of title insurance to be furnished at the seller's expense. A buyer who is asking the seller to pay for the policy may be willing to permit the seller to choose. However, because it is the buyer who must live with the coverage and deal with the insurance company when a title problem surfaces, the buyer may want to be able to pick the title insurance company.

Choice of title company and who pays for title insurance is negotiated by the parties. When the parties have come to an agreement on this matter, check the appropriate box in paragraph 6A.

In addition to identifying who issues and who pays for the title policy, paragraph 6A establishes that the policy is subject to the exclusions promulgated by the state insurance board in Austin, Texas.

The standard printed exception, in paragraph 6A(8), relates to discrepancies, conflicts, and shortages in area or boundary lines. It may be amended to include only shortages in area by providing a **survey** acceptable to the title company and paying an additional fee. Boxes must be checked in paragraph 6A(8) to inform the title company of the intent of the parties regarding the amendment. Check with the title company about the cost of the endorsement and identify who will pay for it (buyer or seller) in paragraph 6A(8) of the contract.

Title Commitment

In paragraph 6B, the agreement calls for the seller to furnish the buyer a **commitment** for title insurance and, at the buyer's expense, legible copies of deed restrictions (restrictive covenants) and documentation of any exceptions in the commitment. This must occur within 20 days after the title company receives a copy of the contract. The seller requests that the title company mail or hand deliver the commitment to the buyer's address shown in paragraph 21 of the contract form. The parties agree that if the title company is unable to deliver within 20 days, the time for delivery is automatically extended up to 15 days or 3 days before the closing date, whichever is sooner.

At this time, double check the names of the sellers, the legal description of the property, and any issue that will not be cleared up at closing. The buyer will want to determine if the seller is retaining any rights (e.g., mineral rights) to the property.

It is important to understand the restrictive covenants and other deed restrictions that are in place for a specific piece of real estate because they dictate how the buyer can and cannot use the property.

Restrictive covenants are deed restrictions that apply to a group of homes or lots in a specific development or subdivision. They are normally put in place by the original developer and are different for every area of homes.

Restrictive covenants nearly always stipulate the minimum size residence allowed, how many homes may be built on one lot, and what type of construction the homes must (or must not) be. Other restrictive covenants include the following:

- Setbacks (how far homes must be from streets and interior lot lines)
- Easements (such as a pathway for power lines or roads)
- Fees for road maintenance or amenities
- Rules regarding changing or voiding the covenants
- Rules about pets and other animals (e.g., no livestock, no unchained pets)
- Regulations dealing with in-home businesses and home rentals
- Rules that limit tree cutting
- Clauses that dictate what type of fencing can be used or that forbid all types of fencing
- Clauses to reduce clutter on lots, such as prohibiting owners from storing a vehicle that doesn't run within view of others, or parking a recreational vehicle on the property

After the buyer receives the commitment, the buyer has some days to object in writing to any matters disclosed in the commitment. The number of days will be determined by agreement of the parties.

Survey and Affidavit

Paragraph 6C of the contract provides for three survey options. If the seller wants to furnish the existing survey, the listing agent must ascertain that the survey is available for the buyer. The contract also calls for the seller to furnish the buyer with a Residential Real Property Affidavit (*see* Figure 4.1), promulgated by the Texas Department of Insurance. The parties negotiate the number of days, after the effective date, that both the affidavit and the survey must be delivered to the buyer.

The best practice is for the seller to get the affidavit signed and notarized, and provide it to the listing agent along with a copy of the survey, soon after listing the property. The listing agent is then in a position to furnish both to the buyer or their agent quickly when an offer arrives. If the seller agrees to paragraph 6C(1), the seller must furnish a survey and the affidavit or the buyer will obtain a new survey at the seller's expense.

If the seller furnishes the survey and the affidavit timely, but the buyer's lender or the title company says that the existing survey is not acceptable, the parties negotiate in paragraph 6C(1) and agree who will pay for a new survey. When using paragraph 6C(1), be sure to check either the seller's or buyer's checkbox to indicate who will pay for the new survey.

Paragraphs 6C(2) and 6C(3) are both for getting a new survey. In C2 the survey is at the buyer's expense, and in C3 it is at the seller's expense.

FIGURE 4.1

Residential Real Property Affidavit

T-47 Residential Real Property Affidavit
(May be Modified as Appropriate for Commercial Transactions)

Date: _____ GF No. _____
Name of Affiant(s): _____
Address of Affiant: _____
Description of Property: _____
County _____, Texas

Title Company as used herein is the Title Insurance Company whose policy of title insurance is issued in reliance upon the statements contained herein.

Before me, the undersigned notary for the State of _____, personally appeared Affiant(s) who after by me being sworn, stated:

1. We are the owners of the Property. (Or state other basis for knowledge by Affiant(s) of the Property, such as lease, management, neighbor, etc. For example, "Affiant is the manager of the Property for the record title owners.")

2. We are familiar with the property and the improvements located on the Property.

3. We are closing a transaction requiring title insurance and the proposed insured owner or lender has requested area and boundary coverage in the title insurance policy(ies) to be issued in this transaction. We understand that the Title Company may make exceptions to the coverage of the title insurance as Title Company may deem appropriate. We understand that the owner of the property, if the current transaction is a sale, may request a similar amendment to the area and boundary coverage in the Owner's Policy of Title Insurance upon payment of the promulgated premium.

4. To the best of our actual knowledge and belief, since _____ there have been no:
    a. construction projects such as new structures, additional buildings, rooms, garages, swimming pools or other permanent improvements or fixtures;
    b. changes in the location of boundary fences or boundary walls;
    c. construction projects on immediately adjoining property(ies) which encroach on the Property;
    d. conveyances, replattings, easement grants and/or easement dedications (such as a utility line) by any party affecting the Property.
EXCEPT for the following (If None, Insert "None" Below:)

5. We understand that Title Company is relying on the truthfulness of the statements made in this affidavit to provide the area and boundary coverage and upon the evidence of the existing real property survey of the Property. This Affidavit is not made for the benefit of any other parties and this Affidavit does not constitute a warranty or guarantee of the location of improvements.

6. We understand that we have no liability to Title Company that will issue the policy(ies) should the information in this Affidavit be incorrect other than information that we personally know to be incorrect and which we do not disclose to the Title Company.

_____

_____

SWORN AND SUBSCRIBED this _____ day of _____, 20_____.

_____

Notary Public

(T-47 Residential Real Property Affidavit)

(P-2)

Objections

The blanks in Paragraph 6D (Objections) are used to list things that the buyer wants to do with the property, that the buyer may not be able to do because of some restriction, easement, or the like.

For example, if the buyer wants to park an RV in the driveway, the deed restrictions may prevent this. Because restrictions that are part of the platted subdivision are not a basis for exception, the buyer would not have protection under the contract unless in paragraph 6D, at the buyer's request, the agent writes, "park an RV in the driveway." This will give the buyer the opportunity to check the deed restrictions and do any other necessary research to determine if the buyer will be able to park the RV.

Another example would be if the buyer intends to put in a swimming pool after closing. Utility easements created by the dedication deed or plat of the subdivision are not a basis for exception, therefore if there is an easement through the back yard, the buyer may not be able to put in a pool. In paragraph 6D, at the buyer's request, the licensee could add, "the addition of a swimming pool in the back yard."

The buyer has a limited number of days to object to things found on the Commitment, Exception Documents, and Survey or they lose the right to object. The items on Schedule C of the Commitment (judgments, tax liens, etc.) must be cleared. Those items are required by the title company and cannot be waived by the buyer not objecting within the time frame.

The closing date can be extended, if necessary, to allow the seller time to cure any timely objections made by the buyer or the lender. After the seller receives the objections, the seller has 15 days to cure them, or the contract is terminated and earnest money is refunded to the buyer unless the buyer waives the objections.

Notice to Prospective Buyer

Paragraph 6E (Title Notices) of the One to Four Family Residential Contract contains notices to the buyer. The notice in 6E(1) is a requirement of the Real Estate License Act. Every licensee is required to give this written notice to every buyer, even if the buyer is getting a title policy. Licensees actually have three ways to give the notice: (1) using any TREC-promulgated contract form, (2) using TAR's Buyer Representation Agreement, or (3) using the separate approved TREC form, Notice to Prospective Buyer.

The Broker-Lawyer Committee and TREC provide a valuable service for the real estate community, and for sellers, by adding the notices to the promulgated forms (Paragraph 6E(1–10)). It puts agents and sellers both on notice of certain legislation that requires disclosure to buyers about a variety of items. Read these items carefully, and remember that paragraph 6E(2) includes check boxes that require a response.

■ PROPERTY CONDITION: INSPECTIONS, ACCEPTANCE, REPAIRS

Paragraph 7 is Property Condition. Paragraph 7A gives the buyer and the buyer's agent the right of access to the property at reasonable times and for inspections. This includes final walk through inspections. The last line makes the seller responsible for immediately turning on utilities and keeping them on during the time the contract is in effect.

Paragraphs 7B and 7C discuss seller's disclosures, including the lead-based paint disclosure.

Property condition is further discussed in paragraphs 7D, E, and F of the promulgated contract forms.

It is important to note that paragraph 7D(1) says, "Buyer accepts the Property As Is." If there are items the buyer wants repaired, select 7D(2) and list those items.

Paragraph 7E confirms that neither the buyer nor the seller is obligated to do lender required repairs. If there are lender-required repairs and neither party agrees to do them, the property will not qualify for the loan and the contract may be terminated by the buyer, and the buyer will receive the earnest money as stated in paragraph B2 of the Third Party Financing Addendum.

Paragraph 7E also gives the buyer the right to terminate, even if the seller agrees to do the lender-required repairs, if the cost of those repairs is going to exceed 5% of the sales price.

If the seller agrees to do any repairs, either in the original offer or later in an amendment, paragraph F explains that any repairs agreed upon will be done by professionals and completed before closing.

The fact the contract says the property is being purchased "as is" does not relieve the seller or licensee from full disclosure about the condition of the property. "As is" indicates the buyer is willing to buy the property for the price they have offered, in the as is condition they can see, subject only to the things listed in paragraph 7D. If they find out new information (for example, on the inspection report) and the seller does not want to repair, the buyer can terminate under their option to terminate in paragraph 23.

Seller's Disclosure and Lead-Based Paint Disclosure

Paragraph 7B discusses the Seller's Disclosure Notice, required by the Texas Property Code, and gives the parties three choices for negotiations.

Sellers can limit their future liability by disclosing everything they know about the property. Even things that have been repaired or replaced may need to be disclosed on the notice.

Paragraph 7B(1) is the easiest disclosure option and probably the best choice. In order for this to be available, the listing agent must have gotten the form completed in advance. Many agents take a blank **seller disclosure** form in their listing packet and get the seller to complete it as soon as they list the property. Then they are ready to provide it when a buyer becomes interested.

Buyers need to review the seller's disclosure notice before making an offer. That way, buyers know what they are making an offer on "in its as is condition" and can negotiate appropriately.

Paragraph 7B(2) is for the buyer's agent who is preparing an offer but has not been able to get a completed seller's disclosure from the listing agent. The buyer

---

Paragraph 7B(1) and 7B(2): Know the buyer's remedies should the seller perform or not perform.

Paragraph 7D: Even though the contract states "as is," this does not prevent the parties from negotiating repairs and treatments. This is true during offer stage through funding of the sale.

can make an offer and ask the seller to provide the notice within a certain number of days. The risk for the seller is that even if the seller delivers the disclosure within the proper time frame, the buyer can terminate the contract, for any reason, within seven days and receive the earnest money back. If the seller never delivers it, the buyer has a right to terminate and receive their earnest money back up to the day of closing.

Paragraph 7B(3) is for the seller who (by law) is not required to furnish the notice. Contrary to popular belief, investors and relocation companies are required to provide the notice. The notice is not required for transactions:

- pursuant to a court order or foreclosure sale;
- by a trustee in bankruptcy;
- to a mortgage by a mortgagor or successor in interest, or to a beneficiary of a deed of trust by a trustor or successor in interest;
- by a mortgagee or a beneficiary under a deed of trust who has acquired the real property at a sale conducted pursuant to a power of sale under a deed of trust or a sale pursuant to a court-ordered foreclosure or has acquired the real property by a deed in lieu of foreclosure;
- by a fiduciary in the course of the administration of a decedent's estate, guardianship, conservatorship, or trust;
- from one co-owner to one or more other co-owners;
- made to a spouse or to a person or persons in the lineal line of consanguinity of one or more of the transferors;
- between spouses resulting from a decree of dissolution of marriage or a decree of legal separation or from a property settlement agreement incidental to such a decree;
- to or from any governmental entity; and
- that transfer new residences of not more than one dwelling unit which have not previously been occupied for residential purposes.

The TREC seller's disclosure (Seller's Disclosure of Property Condition) is an optional form, not a promulgated form. All of the information on this form is required by the Property Code and is also on the TAR Seller's Disclosure form, as well as some of the REALTOR® Associations and some brokers' forms. TAR forms also include additional disclosure items.

Paragraph 7C addresses the possibility of the presence of lead-based paint or lead-based paint hazards. Licensees and sellers must be certain that they follow the Department of Housing and Urban Development (HUD) guidelines with regard to the seller's disclosure of the presence of lead-based paint and/or lead hazards. If the building permits for the construction of the home were issued prior to January 1, 1978, an addendum must be used to comply with the federal regulation to furnish a **lead paint disclosure**. You may use the TREC Form OP-L, Addendum for Seller's Disclosure of Information on Lead-Based Paint, and Lead-Based Paint Hazards as Required by Federal Law (lead paint disclosure form), or the HUD form.

It is important that sellers fill out the lead paint disclosure to the best of their knowledge and sign and date it prior to the buyer signing it. Best practice indicates that the listing agent should include this form in the listing packet with the seller disclosure so it is ready when a buyer becomes interested in the property.

The seller must check one of the boxes in each section of paragraph B of the lead paint disclosure form.

The buyer must check boxes in paragraphs C and D. Paragraph C(2) explains the buyer's right to do inspections within 10 days and right to terminate within 14 days.

The buyer's agent should have furnished the buyer with a booklet called *Protect Your Family from Lead in Your Home*. The buyer acknowledges receipt of the booklet in paragraph D.

Paragraph E of the lead paint disclosure form explains the broker's obligation, including the obligation to maintain a copy of the addendum for at least three years.

Paragraph F certifies that everyone who signs the form, including buyers, sellers, and both agents, is giving information "to the best of their knowledge."

Environmental Matters

Paragraph 7G addresses environmental matters. Buyers should always be given the opportunity to have the property inspected for environmental hazards. Whether their concern is about radon, asbestos, mold, or anything else, the buyer should be satisfied that the property does not pose a health hazard to them or their family.

Always offer the opportunity to use the TREC's Environmental Assessment, Threatened or Endangered Species, and Wetlands Addendum, and structure the transaction with an adequate time frame to accomplish the desired evaluation. The report must get from the inspector to the buyer prior to the agreed period in the option to terminate the contract.

Residential Service Contracts

Paragraph 7H informs the buyer of their right to choose a Residential Service Contract and to negotiate for the seller to reimburse the buyer for the cost. Buyer's agents should make sure the buyer reads the portion of paragraph 7H that is in bold. It is important that the buyer understand the following:

- Many different companies offer service contracts.
- Coverage and exclusions may differ from one company to another.
- It is the buyer's responsibility to review and choose the coverage.

The RESPA prohibits kickbacks (commissions, rebates, referral fees, etc.) for licensees who refer their clients to a particular lender, settlement agent, inspector, residential service company (home warranty company), et cetera, unless the licensee renders a service that warrants a payment or fee. If a licensee is to receive a fee for services rendered, this must be disclosed to the client.

If a licensee refers a client to a residential service provider with whom the licensee has an existing relationship, the licensee should disclose this to the client using TREC's Disclosure of Relationship with Residential Service Company. The form provides for the licensee to disclose any compensation received from the residential service company and the services rendered to earn that compensation.

■ BROKERS' FEES

Paragraph 8: The broker is not a party to the sales contract. Brokers need to have a separate agreement in writing to secure commission (e.g., listing agreement, buyer representation agreement).

Although paragraph 8 is called brokers' fees, brokers' fee agreements are not in the promulgated contract forms. They can be found in the following locations:

■ Listing agreements
■ Buyer representation agreements
■ Agreements between brokers (usually through the MLS system) or by using TAR 2402, Registration Agreement Between Brokers

This will be discussed in greater detail in Chapter 8.

■ SUMMARY

Paragraph 4 provides a place for disclosure if the real estate license holder is a party to the transaction; if the real estate license holder is acting on behalf of a spouse, parent, child, or business entity in which the license holder owns more than 10%; or if the real estate license holder is a trustee for a trust where the beneficiary is the license holder's spouse, parent, or child.

Paragraphs 5 and 6 describe the agreement between the parties regarding earnest money, the title policy, and the survey.

The Broker-Lawyer Committee and TREC provide a valuable service for the real estate community and for sellers by adding the Notices to the promulgated forms in paragraph 6E. The paragraph puts agents and sellers both on notice of certain legislation that requires disclosure to buyers about a variety of items. The buyer receives the notice when they receive the contract form.

Paragraph 7 discusses property condition, including seller's disclosure notice, lead-paint disclosure, environmental matters, and residential service contracts.

Paragraph 8 reminds us that the contractual agreements between the two brokers, the broker and the seller, and the broker and the buyer are all found in other documents. The sales contract is the agreement between the buyer and the seller only.

■ CONTRACT WORKSHOP

1. A buyer checked the box that reads, "This contract is not subject to buyer obtaining buyer approval" in paragraph B1 on the TREC Third Party Financing Addendum. The lender is requiring repairs that will cost several hundred dollars. Is the seller obligated to do the repairs? Is the buyer obligated to do the repairs?
2. According to the TREC One to Four Family Residential Contract, will the cost of the owner's title policy be a buyer expense, a seller expense, or negotiable?
3. The lender is requiring extensive repairs that will cost almost $6,000. The sales price is $90,500. The seller is willing to do the repairs. Is the buyer obligated to continue with the transaction according to the TREC contract?

CHAPTER 4 QUIZ

1. According to the One to Four Family Residential Contract (Resale), the title policy cost is the responsibility of the
   a. party that agreed to pay the cost in the contract.
   b. seller.
   c. buyer.
   d. the lender.

2. The title policy protects the buyer from loss due to utility easements created by the dedication deed or plat of the subdivision.
   a. True
   b. False

3. The buyer will receive a copy of the restrictive covenants at the _____ expense, according to the contract.
   a. seller's
   b. buyer's
   c. title company's
   d. lender's

4. Restrictive covenants may include rules regarding
   a. minimum size requirements.
   b. pets.
   c. fees for road maintenance.
   d. all of these.

5. If the seller furnishes the existing survey to the buyer, but it is NOT acceptable to the buyer's lender, who will cover the cost of a new survey?
   a. Buyer
   b. Lender
   c. Party negotiated in the contract
   d. Seller

6. When the existing survey is NOT acceptable to either the lender or the title company, the buyer shall obtain a new survey no later than _____ days prior to the closing date.
   a. three
   b. five
   c. two
   d. four

7. Buyer must object NOT later than the closing date or within _____ days after receiving the Commitment, Exception Documents, and the survey.
   a. five
   b. three
   c. an agreed-upon number of
   d. seven

8. Provided the seller will NOT incur any expense, how many days after their receipt does the seller have to cure the timely objections of the buyer or any third-party lender?
   a. 3
   b. 5
   c. 15
   d. 7

9. Who has the responsibility for turning on the utilities and keeping them on for the duration of the contract, according to the contract?
   a. Broker
   b. Buyer
   c. Agent
   d. Seller

10. Which of the following are NOT required, according to the Property Code, to furnish a Seller's Disclosure Notice?
    a. Single-family new residences
    b. Property owned by Relocation Companies
    c. Property owned by investors
    d. All of these

CHAPTER

5

Closing, Possession, and More

■ **LEARNING OBJECTIVES** *When you have completed this chapter, you will be able to*

■ **describe** the provisions of the closing and possession paragraphs (paragraphs 9 and 10) of the One to Four Family Residential Contract;

■ **describe** the proper use of the Buyer's and Seller's Temporary Lease Agreements and the importance of holdover fees in paragraph 19 of those agreements;

■ **discuss** what may and may not be included in the Special Provisions paragraph of the One to Four Family Residential Contract;

■ **fill** out paragraph 12 (Settlement and Other Expenses) of the One to Four Family Residential Contract and identify the provisions within it;

■ **identify** the paragraphs in the One to Four Family contract that do not need to be filled out and just describe the rights or agreements of the parties;

■ **describe** how to properly fill out paragraphs 21–24 of the One to Four Family Residential Contract;

■ **discuss** the proper procedure for executing and communicating the acceptance of the One to Four Family Residential Contract; and

■ **describe** the purpose of the final page of the One to Four Family Residential Contract.

■ KEY TERMS

amendment	general warranty deed	seller's expenses
buyer's expenses	lease	specific performance
casualty loss	liquidated damages	temporary residential
closing cost	possession	lease
default	prorations	

■ CLOSING AND POSSESSION

Closing and the buyer's possession of the property are important issues addressed in paragraphs 9 and 10. Closing needs to occur on or before a specific date, while possession should generally be granted at the happening of a defined event, such as closing or funding, or according to a temporary lease agreement promulgated by TREC.

Closing

> Paragraph 9 identifies the closing date and seller's and buyer's performances.

The parties negotiate the closing date in Paragraph 9A. Once the offer is agreed upon, this is an on or before date. So, if the parties agree, they can close earlier but not later. If the closing date needs to be extended, it will require all parties to sign an **amendment** to the contract. The amendment form will be reviewed later.

The only way the closing date may be automatically extended is if objections have been made regarding the commitment and/or the survey (in paragraph 6D).

Paragraph 9B discloses some of the buyer's and the seller's obligation at the time of closing.

The seller is to convey title with a **general warranty deed**.

■ POSSESSION

> Paragraph 10 identifies whether possession of the property happens at funding or according to a lease.

Possession is negotiated in paragraph 10. It is possible to have a transaction in which the buyer takes possession prior to closing or a seller remains in the property for some period after closing. If the parties agree that possession will be other than "upon closing and funding" a temporary **lease** agreement must be used. TREC promulgates two temporary residential leases:

■ Seller's Temporary Residential Lease
■ Buyer's Temporary Residential Lease

The information in the bold letters of paragraph 10 is important for the parties to read. Both need to consult their insurance agent and determine if their interests are protected. For example, if closing takes place on Tuesday, and the seller is still in the property when it is destroyed by fire on Thursday it brings up questions.

■ Because the seller is no longer the owner, their homeowners insurance may no longer exist. Does the seller still have coverage on the personal items in the property?

■ Because the buyer has not moved in yet is the dwelling covered by the buyer's new homeowners' policy?

When a buyer moves in before closing and funding or a seller remains after closing and funding, a landlord/tenant relationship exists. The relationship must be clearly defined by a seller's or buyer's **temporary residential lease** (e.g., TREC's Seller's Temporary Residential Lease or Buyer's Temporary Residential Lease). Failure to use the appropriate temporary lease will create a tenancy at sufferance. Pay particular attention to the provisions relating to insurance coverage on the property during the tenancy period. A temporary lease may not be used to address any tenancy that exceeds 90 days. If the tenancy exceeds 90 days, the owner will need to regard the property as a residential rental property and bring it into compliance with Chapter 92 of the Texas Property Code, the chapter that defines security devices, smoke detectors, and other features that must be provided in a residential rental unit.

■ TEMPORARY LEASE FORMS

When the seller is going to remain in the property after closing, the Seller's Temporary Lease is to be used. The full amount of the daily rental (day after closing and funding to end of lease) and the security deposit is to be paid to the landlord (buyer) at the time of funding of the sale. The security deposit will be refunded after the seller vacates the property.

When the buyer moves in early, the Buyer's Temporary Lease will be used. The full amount of the daily rental (commencement date to closing date) will be paid to landlord (seller) at the time of commencement. Any security deposit will be paid at the same time. The security deposit will be refunded at closing and funding. If the rental period winds up being longer than paid for (e.g., closing was delayed), the difference will be due at funding.

Issues arise when tenants do not vacate as agreed. While this is not an issue for the buyer as tenant when there is a successful close, it could become a real problem if the contract terminates (*see* paragraph 18 of the Buyer's Temporary Lease) and the would-be buyer has to vacate so a new buyer can move in. In both temporary lease agreements, holding over is addressed in paragraph 19, although the paragraphs are slightly different from one form to the next:

■ Paragraph 19 (Holding Over) of Buyer's Temporary Residential Lease states "Any possession by Tenant after termination creates a tenancy at sufferance and will not operate to renew or extend this Lease. Tenant shall pay $_____ per day during the period of any possession after termination as damages, in addition to any other remedies to which Landlord is entitled."

■ Paragraph 19 (Holding Over) of Seller's Temporary Residential Lease has an additional sentence in it (in **bold** in the following passage) The paragraph states "**Tenant shall surrender possession of the Property upon termination of this Lease.** Any possession by Tenant after termination creates a tenancy at sufferance and will not operate to renew or extend this Lease. Tenant shall pay $_____ per day during the period of any possession after termination as damages, in addition to any other remedies to which Landlord is entitled."

Consider the fee for any holdover carefully. The amount of daily holdover should be enough to discourage the tenant from staying. It should be a good business decision for the tenant to go to a hotel rather than pay a holdover fee.

The temporary leases are only good for 90 days. During that period, the landlords are exempt from the requirements of an ordinary lease (fire alarms, windows that lock, etc.). Also, if a lease and a purchase are combined for longer than 90 days, it probably falls under an executory contract under Texas law. There are no approved forms for executory transactions. The parties would need to have an attorney prepare the forms for such a transaction. Licensees should never change the TREC forms to try to make them fit a transaction. If there is no form available, the parties need an attorney.

■ SPECIAL PROVISIONS

| Paragraph 11: Choose your words carefully! |

When the parties need to add factual statements or business details to their agreement, they may use paragraph 11 (Special Provisions). When the parties want to define legal rights and remedies, they should seek competent legal advice. When the parties ask the agents to write language that defines legal rights and remedies, agents should advise them to seek competent legal advice. Licensees are prohibited from including legal rights or remedies in paragraph 11, but buyers/sellers and their attorneys are not.

Factual statements and business details are clarifications of something in the contract. They are true, factual, and simply expand on a subject elsewhere in the contract, not a new negotiation.

Things that can be added in paragraph 11 (by a licensee) include the following:

■ Factual statements and business details applicable to the sale

■ Provisions that cannot fit into a space (e.g., multiple sellers)

The agent should make certain that an offer is properly withdrawn, or the buyer has the right to terminate, before assisting a buyer to make an offer on another property.

Do not write a statement that the buyer's offer is automatically withdrawn at a particular point in time if the seller has not made a response to the offer. This is not a factual statement.

Do not make the offer contingent on the appraisal or the inspection. The inspections are covered by the buyer's option to terminate. If the property does not appraise for the desired value and the lender will not be able to make the loan described in paragraph 3B, the buyer is protected under paragraph B2 of the Third Party Financing Addendum.

TREC Rule §537.11(g) states: A licensee may not add to a promulgated contract form factual statements or business details for which a contract addendum, lease or other form has been promulgated by the commission for mandatory use.

When the provisions are extensive and require more than the space provided, the parties may need to seek the assistance of a competent attorney. The TREC has kept the space small for good reason.

Remember, if TREC provides a promulgated addendum that addresses a situation, the addendum must be used. It is a violation of TREC Rules for an agent to write something in Special Provisions if TREC has an addendum that addresses the situation.

The following are examples of things that may not be addressed in Special Provisions paragraph 11:

- The transaction is contingent upon the sale of another property (use instead the Addendum for Sale of Other Property by Buyer).
- The contract is in a second or back-up position (use instead the Addendum for Back-Up Contract).
- The assumption transaction is contingent upon the seller's release of liability, or in the case of a VA-guaranteed loan, restoration of VA entitlement (use instead the Addendum for Release of Liability on Assumed Loan and/or Restoration of Seller's VA Entitlement).
- The buyer and the seller arrange for the seller to stay after closing or the buyer to possess before closing (use instead Seller's Temporary Residential Lease or Buyer's Temporary Residential Lease).
- The contract is contingent upon satisfactory inspections to the buyer.
- The parties agree that, in the event of a dispute, they will try mediation before bringing a lawsuit.
- The licensee uses wording that defines legal rights and remedies, such as *contingent upon*, *terminate*, *refund earnest money on demand*, *cancel*, and so forth.
- Parties should contact an attorney before using the words *time is of the essence*.
- Agents should never use the words *time is of the essence*.

■ SETTLEMENT AND OTHER EXPENSES

Seller pays on behalf of the buyer "unallowables" and/or buyer's other expenses. Unallowables are lender fees that the borrower is prohibited from paying, so the seller must pay them. FHA and VA loans have unallowables. Also, if the buyer wants the seller to pay for some of the buyer's cost in closing, 12A(1)(b) is where this dollar amount would go.

Paragraph 12 (Settlement and Other Expenses) defines all of the various costs (**closing costs**) and who is responsible for payment (**seller's expenses** and **buyer's expenses**). When you look at all of the buyer's expenses in 12A(2), it is easy to see why sometimes the buyer needs help obtaining the cash for closing.

If the seller is willing to help the buyer with the buyer's cost, in addition to paying the seller's own cost, the amount can be negotiated in 12A(1)(b).

Paragraph 12 not only defines the buyer's and seller's cost, but it also explains that if any cost exceeds an amount one of the parties has agreed to pay, that party can terminate unless the other party agrees to pay the excess.

Agents need to become very familiar with paragraph 12 so that as costs arrive during the transaction they know immediately which party is responsible.

■ PRORATIONS, CASUALTY LOSS, DEFAULT, AND MEDIATION

Paragraph 13: Know how to prorate certain expenses.

Because property taxes in Texas are paid in arrears, many times the tax **prorations** are based on last year's tax amount because the current year's tax amount is not yet available. If, when current amounts are available, there is a variance from what is prorated, paragraph 13 (Prorations) says the parties will work that out on their own.

Take note that items subject to proration in paragraph 13 will be prorated through the day of closing. The seller will be charged the expense for closing day whether the parties close early in the morning or just before the title company closes.

Paragraph 14 (Casualty Loss), makes it clear that the seller is responsible for the property up until the closing date.

> **Paragraph 14:** Know the buyer's choices should the property be damaged prior to funding.

> **Paragraph 15:** Know the remedies of the non-defaulting party.

> **Paragraph 16:** Mediation cost is equally shared among the parties.

Paragraph 15 states that both parties have the same rights if the other party **defaults** under the contract.

Either party may enforce **specific performance** and/or seek such other relief provided by law, or accept the earnest money as **liquidated damages**, releasing everyone under the contract.

Paragraph 16 (Mediation) addresses mediation as a form of dispute resolution. A licensee should have a general understanding of the benefits and limitations of litigation, arbitration, and meditation. In litigation, a judge or a jury will decide the outcome—an outcome that can be appealed to a higher court for consideration. In arbitration, the parties present their positions to a third, disinterested party who listens and then renders a decision that may or may not be binding. The decision reached in arbitration is binding on the parties only if they have contractually agreed that it will be so prior to the arbitration hearing.

Mediation has become the preferred alternative dispute-resolution approach in Texas and has enjoyed a very high success rate. In mediation, a third, disinterested party facilitates communication between the disputing parties to enable them to move toward a point of agreement. The mediator does not need to be a subject area expert. The mediator does not make decisions as to who is right or wrong. A skilled mediator will set the ground rules for the discussions, keep the parties focused by asking probing questions, and help each of the parties listen to what the other party has to say. If the parties reach agreement, they will reduce the agreement to writing and will be legally bound to the new contract that they have created. If they do not reach agreement, they will usually move on to either binding arbitration or litigation.

The four most frequently cited advantages of mediation are the following:

- Low cost
- Fast—much quicker than litigation
- Private—whereas everything that happens or is said in court is public
- Win-win—offering an opportunity for both parties to win

The cost of mediation is shared equally by the parties and can range from a few hundred dollars to $1,500 or more. The fee will be determined by the mediator and will vary, depending on the complexity of the issues, the experience of the mediator, the complexity of the case, and the time involved.

■ ESCROW PROVISIONS

Paragraph 18C (Demand) covers two different situations:

1. Either party can send a release of earnest money form to the other party. If the parties agree on how and to whom the money should be released, and they both sign the release, the escrow agent can release the earnest money.

Paragraph 18 describes the sequence of the release of earnest money.

2. If the parties do not agree, either party can send a written demand to the escrow agent for the money. The escrow agent will then send a copy of the demand to the other party. If, after 15 days, the escrow agent does not receive an objection from the other party, the escrow agent may refund the money to the party making the demand. The expenses that have been incurred on behalf of the party receiving the money will be withheld from the earnest money.

Paragraph 18D relates to the party who wrongfully refuses to sign a release and makes that party liable for damages, plus the earnest money, reasonable attorney's fees, and all costs of the suit.

18E reminds us that all notices must be sent in compliance with paragraph 21.

■ OTHER CONTRACT PROVISIONS

Attorney's Fees

Paragraph 17: Attorney's fees are paid by the buyer or seller who employs the attorney, NOT the real estate licensee.

The wording concerning the attorney's fees (paragraph 17) is straightforward and common in most real estate-related agreements. It appears that the Broker-Lawyer Committee and the TREC intended for the wording to include licensees who might become a party in a legal proceeding brought with respect to the subject transaction. Texas courts have frequently used this paragraph to ascertain that licensees be reimbursed for their legal fees when prevailing in a law suit.

Representations

Paragraph 19. The contractual promises made are forever. The property is NOT off the market during an executory contract.

Paragraph 19 (Representations) says that all representations and warranties will survive closing and reminds the parties that the seller may continue to show the property for back-up offers.

Federal Tax Requirements

Paragraph 20 is Federal Tax Requirements. When closing takes place at a title company, the escrow agent makes certain that Internal Revenue Service (IRS) regulations are followed. The parties should read the paragraph and seek answers to their questions from qualified sources.

Notices

Paragraph 21. Know your broker's policy! Enter the parties' contact information. It's okay to also include the brokerage information but is NOT advisable to include only the brokerage information because it is an opening for legality down the road.

Paragraph 21 is Notices. Ask the buyer and seller where notices are to be mailed, emailed, or transmitted by fax. Texas courts will require validation of a contract evidenced by fax signatures. It is best to obtain the original signature of each of the parties at the signature lines.

Agreement of Parties

Paragraph 22: Do NOT list or attach the IABS, employment agreements, or notices.

Paragraph 22 is Agreement of Parties. Any addenda that are to be a part of the agreement must be identified in the agreement. The TREC has made it very easy for the parties and the agents to make certain that all addenda are listed. Failure to list or reference an addendum in the agreement can cause serious problems. If it is not referenced in the contract, a court is not likely to accept the addendum in question as a part of the agreement.

Do not list the following (these forms are not part of the agreement, they are for information only):

- Seller's disclosure notice
- Information about brokerage services
- The TAR Notification of Intermediary Relationship form

Termination Option

Paragraph 23 (Termination Option) is perhaps the most misunderstood paragraph of the contract. Please note the following:

- There is no right to terminate option if the buyer fails to pay the money to the seller.
- The agreement is for the buyer to pay the seller within three days of the effective date of the contract.
- When the seller accepts the terms and the option fee, the seller should execute the agreement and the seller's receipt that follows on page 9.
- The seller's agent may accept the option fee on behalf of the seller client and sign the receipt. The agent will sign the agent's name. To sign the seller's name would be an act of forgery.
- Days in the contract are calendar days and time is of the essence for this paragraph.

Consult an Attorney

Although paragraph 24 (Consult an Attorney Before Signing) allows it, names of attorneys are not required. They can be included at the request of the parties.

Paragraph 23: Watch the time frame of performance for option fee and option time.

Paragraph 24: Parties can employ an attorney at any time. The agreement is EXECUTED on a date making the offer into an executory contract. Only at time of funding is the agreement an executed contract.

■ EXECUTING THE CONTRACT AND FINALIZING THE AGREEMENT

When the parties sign at the bottom of page eight, the agreement between the parties has been reached.

The broker who obtains the final signatures and/or initials and communicates the acceptance to the other party or the other party's broker must fill out the executed date. A licensee working for the broker may fill out the executed date on the broker's behalf.

Four things have to happen to have an executed date.

1. The agreement is in writing and signed by all parties.
2. All changes have been initialed.
3. The agreement is clear and includes unambiguous language.
4. The fact that the contract is accepted has been communicated to the other party or the other party's agent.

Delivering the Money

Usually the licensee obtains two checks from the prospective buyer when writing the offer: one for the earnest money made payable to the escrow or title company and one for the option money made payable to the seller. Good business practice says that the buyer's agent hold on to those checks until the contract is finalized.

Once the offer is accepted and there is an effective date, the agent holding the checks has critical time restraints to get them delivered. The Rules of the Commission says earnest money must be to the escrow agent by the close of business on the second day after the effective date, and the contract says the option money must be to the seller, or their agent, within three days after the effective date.

■ AMENDMENT

Once a contract has been fully executed, that document can no longer be changed. After a contract is executed, all changes must be done with the promulgated amendment (Amendment to Contract). The sales contract has an executed date and each amendment has its own executed date, providing a history of the original agreement and the date it happened, along with dates of any further changes.

■ THE LAST PAGE

Page 9 of the contract is for information only. The buyer's and the seller's signatures completed the agreement between the parties at the end of page 8.

Broker Information

The final page of the contract asks for the name of, and other information for, the licensed supervisor. That is either the licensee, given the authority to monitor the agents' business practices by the Broker of Record, or the Broker of Record.

§535.2(e).   Broker's Responsibility of the Rules of the Texas Real Estate Commission states the following:

> "A broker may designate another licensee to assist in administering compliance with the Act and the Rules, but the Broker may not relinquish overall responsibility for the supervision of licensees sponsored by the broker. Any such designation must be in writing."

Option Fee Receipt

Paragraph 23 of the contract says that the buyer's option fee will be delivered to the seller within three days of the effective date of the contract. If it is delivered to an agent in the listing broker's office, legally it has been delivered to the seller. One of the ways to prove delivery within the proper time frame is the Option Fee Receipt on page 9 of the contract. If proof is provided in another manner (for example a receipt for certified mail) it is not necessary to use the receipt on page 9 of the sales contract.

Contract and Earnest Money Receipt

The buyer's agent should deposit the contract and earnest money, if any, to the escrow agent immediately and obtain a receipted copy of the contract for all affected parties.

Note that the receipt is issued by the escrow agent, not the listing or selling licensee. Some escrow agents may choose to use their own receipt form for the contract and the earnest money instead of the form at the end of the contract.

Brokers and salespersons are reminded that the TREC rules require that the licensee deposit the earnest money with the escrow agent by the close of business on the second business day of the escrow company after the execution of the contract by the principals. The only exception occurs when the principals agree that a deposit may be delayed and a different time is expressly defined in paragraph 11 of the contract (Rule 535.146).

■ SUMMARY

Paragraphs 9 through 24 cover the agreement of the parties regarding:

■ Closing
■ Possession
■ Use of temporary lease agreements when possession is different from closing
■ Closing cost for both the buyer and the seller
■ Default and the remedies
■ Mediation
■ The buyer's right to terminate

Paragraph 11 gives space to add factual statements and business details (desired by the principals) to the agreement. The licensee must be careful not to add anything that could be considered changing legal rights.

The parties sign the agreement at the bottom of page 8 of the One to Four Family Residential Contract. The bottom of page 8 is the end of the agreement between buyer and seller. Page 9 is strictly for information. Nothing on page 9 is an agreement to anything. The agreement between brokers is found either in MLS or a separate written agreement.

Any changes to the agreement after the executed date must be done using the amendment.

■ CONTRACT WORKSHOP

1. The lender is requiring an inspection by an electrician. Who will pay for that inspection?
2. A property is to close on October 12. On October 11, the buyer goes to the property for a final walk-through inspection and finds the property has been vandalized. Is the buyer responsible for the repairs?
3. A contract was negotiated with paragraph 6C2 checked. The Title Company ordered the survey. The contract did not close. The seller made a written demand for the earnest money. The Title Company notified the buyer that the seller was requesting the earnest money. The buyer never responded to the Title Company. Thirty-five days later, the Title Company plans to send a check to the seller. According to the contract, will the title company withhold the fee for the survey from the seller's funds?
4. ABC Realty is acting as an intermediary in a transaction, and they have appointed two different agents to assist the principals. The names of both agents from ABC should be on the contract. Where should the names be on the form? What should it say in Agreement between Brokers?

5. The Third Party Financing Addendum indicated that the total adjusted origination fees were not to exceed 2%. Paragraph 12A(1)(b) indicated that the seller would pay 2% for that amount. The discount changed drastically, and now, the fees are 3%. According to the contract, if the seller agrees to pay the excess, can the buyer terminate the contract? If the buyer agrees to pay the excess, can the seller terminate the contract? If the buyer agrees to split the excess with the seller, is the seller obligated to agree?

6. Should the Seller's Disclosure Notice be listed in paragraph 22 of the TREC contract?

7. If a buyer fills in the blanks in paragraph 23, in the TREC One to Four Family Residential Contract, but four days after the effective date the money has not been received by the seller or the seller's agent, what is the status of the contract?

■ TRANSACTION: STRASSMAN TO APPLEWHITE

Refer to Texas Promulgated Forms Supplement for the forms needed for this case study.

William Applewhite and his wife, Sharon, are unable to qualify for a new loan because they are newly self-employed. They currently live at 1504 Center Ct, Apt 1001, Plano, TX 75093. They call on one of your listings that advertises seller financing.

The property is located at 1233 Tree Lane in Plano, Texas 75093. You show the property to the Applewhites, and they are excited. They have received and reviewed the Seller's Disclosure Notice. The property meets all of their needs. They want to make a full-price offer.

The seller, Robert Strassman, is a single man who bought the home new in 1984 and is still living in the property. The legal description of the property is Lot 20, Block 15 in the Edwards Lake Subdivision in Collin County. There is a mandatory homeowners association requiring a $100 transfer fee and a $50-a-month assessment. The buyer wants to examine the homeowners association documents and the Resale Certificate prior to closing; these are to be provided by the seller within five days after the effective date of the contract. The seller wants to examine a credit report for the buyer before final acceptance of the offer and ask the buyer to provide it within three days after the effective date.

The buyer wants a Residential Service Policy and wants the seller to reimburse them for $375.

The asking price is $250,000, and the seller wants 10% down and will carry the note at 5% interest for 15 years. The principal and interest payments will be $1,779.29. Taxes on the property will be $7,400 with no exemptions, and insurance will run $1,725 a year. The seller wants to hold an escrow account for taxes and insurance. The seller wants to reserve the right to approve any future buyers wanting to assume the seller financing.

The buyers are willing to put up the entire down payment as escrow money with Ticor Title Company at 1010 San Pedro Road in Frisco, Texas. The closer will be Mary Jane Smite. The buyers really want a new survey within 10 days and want the seller to pay for it. They want a seven-day option period and are willing to pay $275 for the option fee. They want it to be credited to the sales price at closing. Neither party has an attorney. The seller is willing to pay for the owners' title policy and for an amendment to change the standard printed exception on the title policy to shortages in area only.

The parties agree to a three-day time period to object after the buyer receives the Commitment, Exception Documents, and Survey.

You have a 7% Listing Agreement with the seller, and the buyer has signed a Buyers Representation Agreement with you. You will be acting as an intermediary representative in the transaction.

They buyers would like to close on the 28th of next month and are willing to allow the seller to stay in the property for three days after closing. The parties agree that the interest on the seller financing will begin three days after closing and funding in lieu of daily rent. The buyers want a $2,500 deposit to secure performance of the lease. The parties agree to a daily holdover amount of $1,000.00

Other information you will need:

- The name of the HOA is Arbor HOA and the telephone number is 214-854-1689
- The Applewhites' telephone number is 214-797-6501 and email address is wapplewhite@verizon.net
- Robert Strassman's telephone number is 214-505-1904 and email address is robert.strassman@gmail.com

Complete the offer.

CHAPTER 5 QUIZ

1. If the tenant damages the property while occupying, the cost of repair is the responsibility of the
   a. landlord.
   b. broker.
   c. tenant.
   d. agent.

2. According to paragraph 12, seller's expenses include
   a. discount fees.
   b. tax certificates.
   c. mortgagee title policy.
   d. both b. and c.

3. If a closing takes place in July, who will be responsible for payment of the annual taxes to the taxing authority when the tax statements arrive?
   a. Seller
   b. Buyer
   c. Title company
   d. Each party will pay their share for the year

4. If one of the parties default and the non-defaulting party accepts the earnest money as damages, that party
   a. may also sue for specific damages.
   b. may also sue for other damages.
   c. can do nothing more; the contract is terminated.
   d. both a. and b.

5. According to paragraph 18B, if no closing occurs, the title company may require
   a. unpaid expenses on behalf of the buyer.
   b. unpaid expenses on behalf of the seller.
   c. a written release of liability of escrow agent.
   d. all of the above.

6. If the escrow agent receives a demand for the earnest money from one party, the escrow agent will send a copy of the demand to the other party. If the escrow agent does *NOT* receive a written objection within ___ days, the escrow agent may release the earnest money to the party making the demand.
   a. 30
   b. 15
   c. 45
   d. 7

7. If one of the parties wrongfully refuses to sign a release acceptable to the escrow agent within _____ days of receipt of the request for the release, they will be liable to the other party for damages, plus the earnest money, reasonable attorney's fees, and all costs of the suit.
   a. 7
   b. 10
   c. 12
   d. 15

8. Notices from one party to the other are effective when they are sent to
   a. the parties' agents.
   b. the email address listed in paragraph 21.
   c. the address listed in paragraph 21.
   d. both b. and c.

9. According to paragraph 23 the option money is to be delivered to the
   a. buyer's agent.
   b. title company.
   c. mail box.
   d. seller.

10. If the option money is *NOT* delivered to the proper party within the proper time frame, what is the status of the contract?
    a. The contract is void.
    b. The contract is voidable.
    c. The contract is valid; paragraph 23 is not a part of the contract.
    d. The contract and paragraph 23 are valid as long as the money is eventually received.

CHAPTER 6

The Remaining Promulgated Forms

■ **LEARNING OBJECTIVES**   *When you have completed this chapter, you will be able to*

■ **identify** the ways in which the other five promulgated contracts differ from the One to Four Family Residential Contract;

■ **describe** the proper use of the Residential Condominium Contract;

■ **describe** the proper use of the Farm and Ranch Contract;

■ **describe** the proper use of the Unimproved Property Contract; and

■ **describe** the proper use of the New Home Contracts.

■ KEY TERMS

completed construction	R-value	surface leases
incomplete construction	rollback tax	timber interests
mineral rights	royalties	water rights

■ INTRODUCTION

As discussed in Chapter 2, TREC promulgates six contract forms:

- Unimproved Property Contract
- One to Four Family Residential Contract (Resale)
- New Home Contract (Incomplete Construction)
- New Home Contract (Completed Construction)
- Farm and Ranch Contract
- Residential Condominium Contract (Resale)

This book has dissected the One to Four Family Residential Contract. While all six of the contracts are similar, there are important differences worth noting that will be discussed in this chapter.

■ IS IT DIFFERENT FROM THE ONE TO FOUR FAMILY CONTRACT?

Generally speaking, only 7 paragraphs contain information different from the One to Four Family Residential Contract:

- Paragraph 2 is different in each contract, describing the type of property that is covered.
- Paragraph 3 is only different in the Farm and Ranch Contract because the sales price can be adjusted by the survey.
- Paragraph 6 is different in Condominium Contract and the Farm and Ranch Contract. The Farm and Ranch Contract allows for information regarding Exception Documents and Surface Leases. Paragraph 6G7 discusses Texas Agricultural Development Districts.
- Paragraph 7 is different in both New Home Contracts, the Unimproved Property Contract, and the Farm and Ranch Contract. Different seller's disclosures are required by the type of property and are contained in these paragraphs.
- Paragraph 12 is only different in the Condominium Contract. It addresses association fees and deposits.
- Paragraph 13 is different in both New Home Contracts, the Unimproved Property Contract, the Farm and Ranch Contract, and the Condominium Contract, but for different reasons.
  - For New Home Contracts, the Unimproved Property Contract, and the Farm and Ranch Contract, there is a possibility of the assessment of rollback taxes. Rollback taxes can be assessed when the property zoning is changing. The amount of roll back taxes can be a significant amount. The contract forms say the party changing the usage is responsible for the roll back assessment. Encourage the parties to investigate and understand roll back taxes and the amount of the assessment before agreeing to be responsible for them.
  - In paragraph 13, the Condominium Contract states the following: "Cash reserves from regular condominium assessments for deferred maintenance or capital improvements established by the Association will not be credited to Seller. Any special condominium assessment due and unpaid at closing will be the obligation of Seller."
- Paragraph 14 is different only in the Condominium Contract. The seller owns the unit only, so that must be defined.

■ RESIDENTIAL CONDOMINIUM CONTRACT

Pay particular attention to paragraphs 2, 6D, 12, 13, and 14 in reviewing the form (Residential Condominium Contract [Resale]).

The Residential Condominium Contract (Resale) is very similar to the One to Four Family Residential Contract, with the exception of the unique provisions relating solely to condominium transactions and the statutory requirements of the Texas Uniform Condominium Act, chapters 81 and 82 of the Texas Property Code.

A study of paragraph 2 will reveal the primary differences between the condominium form and the single-family form that you have studied. Another significant difference is found in paragraph 6 where the survey provisions have been deleted.

As stated earlier, paragraphs 12, 13, and 14 are also different from the One to Four Family Residential Contract.

■ FARM AND RANCH CONTRACT

Pay particular attention to paragraphs 2, 3, 6, 7, and 13 in reviewing the form (Farm and Ranch Contract).

The Farm and Ranch Contract calls for a metes-and-bounds legal description rather than reference to a recorded plat. When selling a farm or ranch property, the parties must address issues and items that are not considerations in the other types of properties addressed by TREC-promulgated forms. These elements include the following:

- Crops
- Equipment
- **Royalties**
- **Surface leases**
- Other restrictions and exceptions already existing or to be created
- Rights and obligations of applicable government programs and cooperative or association memberships

Paragraph 2F of the Farm and Ranch contract says that any reservation for oil, gas or other minerals, water, and timber is made in accordance with an attached addendum or special provisions. Good business practice is that the licensee should use the TREC-promulgated Addendum for Reservation of Oil, Gas and Other Minerals. If the parties want more detailed description of the reservation, they should be advised to seek advice from an oil and gas attorney.

A unique feature of the contract is the provision in paragraph 3 that allows for an adjustment to the sales price based on the results of the survey that may be done after the effective date of the contract. The contract caps the adjustment at 10% of the sales price and gives either party the ability to terminate the agreement if the needed adjustment exceeds that amount.

Paragraph 13 discusses rollback taxes. A **rollback tax** is an additional tax that is collected when an agriculture-use property is no longer used for agricultural purposes and no longer qualifies for a reduced tax rate. When the use of the property is changed to a nonagricultural use, the difference between the reduced agricultural rate and the higher non-agricultural rate must be paid for a statutory number of years prior to the year of the change in use. On an expensive parcel of land, the difference in tax can amount to a very significant amount of money. The buyer and seller must come to an agreement about who will pay the rollback taxes. The obligations imposed by their agreement in the contract will survive closing.

■ UNIMPROVED PROPERTY CONTRACT

Pay particular attention to paragraphs 2, 6D, 7, and 13 in reviewing the form (Unimproved Property Contract).

Due to the lack of fixtures and accessories found in an unimproved property, paragraph 2 of the unimproved property form is considerably less involved and complicated than some paragraphs found in the other forms. A buyer of an unimproved building lot must carefully research zoning ordinances, restrictive covenants, availability of utilities, access, and other matters that will affect the suitability of the building lot for the buyer's intended use. An adequate termination option should be purchased to provide a sufficient amount of time to make absolutely certain that the property is suitable.

■ NEW HOME CONTRACTS

Property owners can instruct licensees to use a form preferred by the owner rather than a TREC-promulgated form. Most builders will require the contract form that they provide. New homes may be sold using one of two TREC forms when the builder does not specify. The TREC Forms that address two types of new homes are as follows:

- **Completed construction** (usually spec homes)— New Home Contract (Complete Construction)
- **Incomplete construction**— New Home Contract (Incomplete Construction)

Carefully review paragraphs 2, 7, and 13, and the notice on page 8 of the form, regarding Chapter 27 of the Texas Property Code and construction defects.

Each of the two forms will have different considerations and issues to be addressed, particularly in paragraph 2, Property, and paragraph 7, Property Condition.

Federal law requires that builders reveal to the buyer the **R-value** of the insulation installed in the new home. This may be included in the contract or in an addendum attached to the contract. The TREC-promulgated contracts address the R-factors in the Property condition paragraph. Other topics that should be addressed include the following:

- Construction documents
- Cost adjustments
- Buyer selections
- Completion dates
- Possible delays
- Warranties

It is always prudent for a buyer to seek legal counsel before signing a builder's contract or before agreeing to the provisions of a contract that addresses incomplete construction. An already completed home in the builder's inventory should be treated in the same manner as a previously occupied resale home with regard to inspections and evaluations by competent professionals. A buyer should never assume that everything in a new home is properly installed and working properly.

A licensee who fails to advise the client to seek the counsel of other professionals is not demonstrating minimum standards of care required by the TREC rules and the fiduciary duties owed to clients.

■ SUMMARY

TREC promulgates six contract forms. The most frequently used is the One to Four Family Residential Contract (Resale). The others address the sale of farms/ranches, condominiums, completed construction, incomplete construction, and unimproved property.

All six contract forms contain much of the same information. The differences address the nuances of dealing with the sale of different types of property.

■ TRANSACTION: TOMAS TO PERRY

Refer to Texas Promulgated Forms Supplement for the forms needed for this case study.

Richard Tomas, a single man, will sell his farm to Thomas Perry and his wife, Anna. The farm has approximately 175 acres. The legal description is a long metes-and-bounds description and is on Exhibit A, which will be an attachment to the purchase agreement. The property is otherwise known as 3013 Rural Lane, City of Paris, Fannin County, Texas. It is not located in the Texas Agricultural Development District or subject to any government programs. Mr. Tomas currently occupies the property. His telephone number is 917-624-1701, and his email address is rtomas@gmail.com.

The Perrys currently live at 1015 Sparkman Ave in Allen, TX 75002 and intend to pay $447,500 cash for the property. The buyers want the seller to provide them with a title policy and a new survey at the seller's expense. They will pay $100,000 earnest money to Fannin County Title and Abstract Company at 1012 Midpoint, Paris, Texas. Closing will take place in 30 days. Possession will be at closing and funding. They would like to have the new survey within 20 days after the effective date and have 7 days to review the survey and the title documents. The buyer does want the title policy standard printed exception changed to shortages in area and is willing to pay for the amendment. The Perrys' telephone number is 294-725-1524 and email address is tomandanna@theperrys.com.

If the survey finds the property to be more or less than the 175 acres, estimated by the seller, the sales price will be adjusted based on $250 per acre.

Mr. Tomas's family has owned the property for many years and has never sold or leased any of the sub-surface rights. Mr. Tomas wants to keep 50% of the gas and oil interest in the property. There are no farm and ranch accessories included in the sale. Mr. Tomas has never leased any part of the property and there are no exception documents.

The usage is not changing as the Perrys intend to continue using the property as agricultural property. There are no crops included in the sale. The Perrys can pay their own closing cost but are going to ask the seller to reimburse them up to $500 to purchase a residential service policy.

The buyers have reviewed the seller's disclosure notice. They have no intention of doing inspections and have waived their right to do inspections for lead-based paint. They are not asking for an option to terminate but do want 20 days to have environmental inspections done.

You are the agent representing the buyer. There is no listing agreement as Mr. Tomas had only mentioned one time that he may be willing to sell. He said he would be willing to pay a 4.5% commission. Suddenly, the Perrys arrived in your office and signed a Buyer's Representation Agreement with you. They made it clear, however, that they would pay no commission out of their pocket (check out the commission agreement on the last page of the Farm and Ranch Contract).

Ken Dunlap at Fannin County Title and Abstract will be the closer on the property. Ken's telephone number is 787-256-4900 and fax is 787-256-4902. His email address is ken@fannintitleandabstract.com

Use this information to complete the offer.

CHAPTER 6 QUIZ

1. Rollback taxes are discussed in
   a. both New Home Contracts.
   b. Unimproved Property Contract.
   c. Farm and Ranch Contract.
   d. all of the above.

2. Rollback taxes can be assessed when
   a. property values are increasing quickly.
   b. property values have been reappraised.
   c. zoning is changing and the property no longer qualifies for a previous exemption.
   d. tax rates have been upgraded.

3. When a buyer purchases a condominium, they are buying the
   a. unit and an undivided interest in the common areas.
   b. unit and the lot.
   c. stock in the company that owns the condominium building.
   d. unit, the lot, and an undivided interest in the common areas.

4. The seller on unimproved property provides a disclosure
   a. on the Sellers' Disclosure of property condition.
   b. in paragraph 7E of TREC 9-10, Unimproved Property Contract.
   c. verbally.
   d. never, because no disclosure is provided in TREC contract forms.

5. Paragraph 6G8 of the Farm and Ranch Contract informs the consumer that if the property is subject to a private transfer fee,
   a. the seller must notify the buyer.
   b. the agent must notify the buyer.
   c. the title company must notify the buyer.
   d. notification is not needed as it is public information.

6. The TREC contract forms that discuss rollback taxes say that if the rollback taxes are assessed because the seller changed the usage prior to closing,
   a. the developer will be obligated to pay the rollback taxes.
   b. the seller will be obligated to pay the rollback taxes.
   c. the buyer will be obligated to pay the rollback taxes.
   d. there will be no rollback taxes.

7. The TREC contract forms say that if the property is damaged by fire or other casualty prior to closing, the
   a. buyer may terminate the contract as is.
   b. buyer is obligated to restore the property after closing.
   c. buyer must accept an assignment of the insurance funds.
   d. seller will be obligated to restore the property prior to closing.

8. Which TREC-promulgated contract form allows for the sales price to be adjusted because of the survey?
   a. The One to Four Family Contract
   b. The Unimproved Property Contract
   c. The Farm and Ranch Contract
   d. The New Home Contract-Complete Construction

9. Which TREC-promulgated contract form(s) gives disclosure about the type of insulation in the property?
   a. The One to Four Family Contract
   b. The Unimproved Property Contract
   c. The Farm and Ranch Contract
   d. Both New Home Contracts

10. Which TREC-promulgated contract form has a spot for information about Exception Documents and Surface Leases?
    a. The One to Four Family Contract
    b. The Unimproved Property Contract
    c. The Farm and Ranch Contract
    d. The New Home Contract-Complete Construction

CHAPTER

Promulgated Addenda, Notices, and Other Forms

■ **LEARNING OBJECTIVES** *When you have completed this chapter, you will be able to*

■ **describe** the proper use of the Addendum for Sale of Other Property by Buyer;

■ **describe** the proper use of the Addendum for Back-Up Contract;

■ **describe** the proper use of the Addendum for Reservation of Oil, Gas, and Other Minerals;

■ **identify** which form a buyer should use to reserve the right to terminate a contract, and describe how mutual termination of a contract should be handled;

■ **describe** the proper use of the Addendum for Property Located Seaward of the Gulf Intracoastal Waterway and the Addendum for Coastal Area Property;

■ **describe** the proper use of the Addendum for Property Subject to Mandatory Membership in an Owner's Association;

■ **describe** the proper use of the Short Sale Addendum;

■ **describe** the proper use of the noncontract forms:
— Promulgated Resale Certificates,
— Consumer Information Form, and
— Information About Brokerage Services Form; and

■ **describe** the proper use of the Non-Realty Items Addendum.

■ KEY TERMS

back-up contract   short sale

■ INTRODUCTION

Many addenda and other forms have already been addressed in this book. This chapter will discuss the remaining promulgated addenda and other TREC forms.

■ ADDENDUM FOR SALE OF OTHER PROPERTY BY BUYER

The Addendum for Sale of Other Property by Buyer is the form to use if the buyers will be unable to buy the new property unless their existing property is sold and closed. It is usually used when the buyer needs the money from the first sale to complete the second sale, but it could be necessary because the new lender would not approve the loan on the new property until the debt is paid in full on the existing loan.

Paragraph A gives a date by which the funds from the sale of the existing property must be received. Paragraph E states, "time is of the essence."

This addendum works best when the buyer's present home is already under contract and they are just concerned about closing and funding.

Remember that paragraph 19 of the promulgated contract form says that the seller can continue to market the property for back-up offers and receive, negotiate, and accept a back-up offer. Paragraph B in this addendum discusses what will happen if the seller accepts a back-up offer.

If the seller accepts a back-up offer, the seller will notify this buyer (buyer 1), and buyer 1 may waive the contingency on or before a date they have agreed upon; otherwise, this first contract will terminate. Paragraph D cautions the buyer not to waive the contingency unless they are certain they can close even if their first property does not close. Otherwise the buyer will be in default.

The parties can agree upon an amount of additional earnest money that must be put up if and when buyer 1 waives the contingency in paragraph C.

■ ADDENDUM FOR BACK-UP CONTRACT

A **back-up contract** enables the seller to negotiate with a second buyer and agree upon terms that will be used for the back-up buyer in the event the first buyer's transaction falls through. The TREC addendum (Addendum for Back-Up Contract) allows for just one back-up.

This addendum can be win-win for both the back-up buyer and the seller, when the back-up buyer is interested in a property that already has a finalized contract with a different buyer.

It is a win for the back-up buyer because if the first contract terminates for any reason, the back-up buyer does not have to compete with other buyers for the home. They have the primary contract now in place. The back-up buyer is free to continue to look for homes; and if they find one they like (as long as they have negotiated for an option to terminate in paragraph 23 of the contract), they can terminate at any time.

It is a win for the seller, who is free to continue to work with the first buyer in a good faith attempt at getting to closing, but now has the power of knowing there is another buyer interested in the property.

Paragraph A simply says that the back-up buyer is going to put up the earnest money and the option money and wait to see if the first transaction terminates. So, in the case of a back-up, the parties negotiate the contract and execute it, the back-up buyer deposits the earnest money with the escrow agent and pays the option money to the seller, and then the parties wait to see what happens with the first buyer.

Paragraphs B and C make several points:

- If the first contract does not terminate by the deadline negotiated by the parties, this back-up contract will terminate and the earnest money will be refunded to the buyer.
- The seller is free to continue to work with the first buyer; an amendment of the first contract does not terminate the first contract.
- If the first contract does terminate, the seller must notify the back-up buyer immediately.
- The effective date of the back-up contract is amended to the date the back-up buyer receives notification of termination of the first contract.

Paragraph D relates that if the back-up buyer has an option to terminate, it

- begins on the original effective date of the back-up contract; and
- continues after the amended effective date for the number of days agreed to in paragraph 23 of the contract.

Paragraph E relays that time is of the essence.

LEARNING CHECK

A back-up contract was originally executed on April 19. The parties agreed to a 10-day option period in paragraph 23. On April 25, the buyer received the notice from the seller that the first contract has terminated.

When does the buyer's option period end?

At 5:00 pm on _____. (Fill in the blank)

■ ADDENDUM FOR RESERVATION OF OIL, GAS, AND OTHER MINERALS

The Addendum for Reservation of Oil, Gas, and Other Minerals was adopted by TREC in 2008 in response to new issues in the marketplace. In addition to using the addendum, the parties should be advised to seek competent legal counsel before finalizing a transaction in which the seller retains oil, gas, or other mineral interests.

■ NOTICE OF BUYER'S TERMINATION OF CONTRACT

The Notice of Buyer's Termination provides a method for the buyer to terminate in five different rights they have under the contract. For example, to exercise the unrestricted right to terminate (as is provided in paragraph 23 of the promulgated contract form), the buyer must deliver the promulgated notice, Notice of Buyer's Termination of Contract, to the seller prior to expiration of the option period. Failure to deliver the notice means that the buyer is obligated to close the transaction according to the terms of the contract.

■ MUTUAL TERMINATION OF CONTRACT

Sometimes the buyer and seller agree that they want to terminate the contract and agree on how the earnest money will be distributed. TAR 1904 is a Release of Earnest Money Form that has language that releases everyone from the contract. Most title companies also have forms available for this purpose. The important thing to remember is that termination of the obligations under the contract are one issue and release of the earnest money is a separate issue. Be sure the form you are using addresses the issues the parties have agreed upon.

■ ADDENDUM FOR PROPERTY LOCATED SEAWARD OF THE GULF INTRACOASTAL WATERWAY

The Addendum for Property Located Seaward of the Gulf Intracoastal Waterway contains the notice required by TEX NR. CODE ANN. § 61.025: Texas Statutes—Section 61.025: DISCLOSURE TO PURCHASER OF PROPERTY. The statute states:

> (a) Except as provided by Subsection (b), a person who sells or conveys an interest, other than a mineral, leasehold, or security interest, in real property located seaward of the Gulf Intracoastal Waterway to its southernmost point and then seaward of the longitudinal line also known as 97 degrees, 12', 19" which runs southerly to the international boundary from the intersection of the centerline of the Gulf Intracoastal Waterway and the Brownsville Ship Channel must include [the statement] in any executory contract for conveyance...
>
> (b) If the statement is not included in the executory contract for conveyance or there is no executory contract for conveyance, the statement must be delivered to, and receipt thereof acknowledged by, the purchaser not later than 10 calendar days prior to closing the transaction.
>
> (c) Failure to comply with Subsection (a) or (b), as applicable, shall be grounds for the purchaser to terminate the contract or agreement to convey, and upon termination any earnest money shall be returned to the party making the deposit.
>
> (d) A seller commits a deceptive act under Section 17.46, Business & Commerce Code, if the seller fails to comply with Subsection (a) or Subsection (b), as applicable.
>
> (e) This section, or the failure of a person to give or receive the notice in the manner required by this section, does not diminish or modify the

beach access and use rights of the public acquired through statute or under common law.

■ ADDENDUM FOR COASTAL AREA PROPERTY

The Addendum for Coastal Area Property contains the notice required by TEX NR. CODE ANN. § 33.135: Texas Statutes—Section 33.135: NOTICE TO PURCHASER OR GRANTEE OF COASTAL AREA PROPERTY. The statute states, in part:

> *A person who sells, transfers, or conveys an interest other than a mineral, leasehold, or security interest in real property adjoining and abutting the tidally influenced waters of the state must include the…notice as a part of a written executory contract for the sale, transfer, or conveyance.*
>
> *If [the] property…is sold, transferred, or conveyed without an executory contract for conveyance, a written statement containing the notice… must be delivered to the grantee for execution and acknowledgement of receipt before the conveyance is recorded.*
>
> *Failure to include the statement in an executory contract for conveyance shall be grounds for the purchaser to terminate such contract, and upon termination any earnest money shall be returned to the party making the deposit.*
>
> *Failure to provide this statement prior to closing, either in the executory contract for conveyance or in a separate written statement, shall constitute a deceptive act under Section 17.46, Business & Commerce Code.*

■ ADDENDUM FOR PROPERTY SUBJECT TO MANDATORY MEMBERSHIP IN AN OWNER'S ASSOCIATION

Paragraph 6E(2) of the One to Four Family Residential Contract addresses the issue of mandatory membership in an owner's association. If the buyer is concerned about what this entails, use the Addendum for Property Subject to Mandatory Membership in an Owner's Association.

This addendum allows the buyer to elect to receive or not to receive the Subdivision Information. As defined in the addendum, *Subdivision Information* means "(i) the restrictions applying to the subdivision, (ii) the bylaws and rules of the Property Owners Association (Association), and (iii) a resale certificate, all of which comply with Section 207.003 of the Texas Property Code."

If the buyer wants to receive the subdivision information, the TREC form Subdivision Information, including Resale Certificate for Property Subject to Mandatory Membership in a Property Owners' Association, can be used for this purpose. This resale certificate is discussed in the next section. This resale certificate is not to be filled out by licensees and is not to be used for condominium transactions.

Paragraph E of the addendum provides authorization from the seller for the association to provide information as needed to the buyer, broker, or title company. If the buyer does not require the information but it is needed by the title company, the title company must collect the cost of obtaining the information prior to obtaining the information. It is necessary when completing the addendum for the agent to select the correct box in paragraph E to give notice to the title company which party will pay this fee.

■ SHORT SALE ADDENDUM

The Short Sale Addendum was also adopted by TREC in 2008. This addendum must be used when structuring a short sale transaction.

A **short sale** transaction cannot move forward without the approval and cooperation of the lender's Loss Mitigation Department. The listing agent and the sellers must contact the lender for permission and directions. Without the lender's cooperation, a short sale transaction cannot and will not close. To avoid wasting everyone's time and efforts, the listing agent should contact the lender early and then make certain that everyone follows the lender's instructions precisely.

■ NONCONTRACT FORMS

The forms that follow are published by the TREC to address important issues and concerns, but they are not a part of any contractual agreement between buyer and seller.

Promulgated Resale Certificates

As mentioned earlier, the TREC form Subdivision Information, including Resale Certificate for Property Subject to Mandatory Membership in an Owners' Association, is used if a property is subject to mandatory membership in a property owners association, and the buyer wants more information about the membership and subdivision information. This is not to be used for condominium transactions.

Paragraph 2C of the Residential Condominium Contract (Resale) addresses the use of the Condominium Resale Certificate.

A representative of the home or property owners association fills out these resale certificates, generally for a fee.

Although licensees do not complete the resale certificates, they should be thoroughly familiar with the content of them.

Consumer Information Form

TREC's Consumer Information Form is to be prominently displayed in the office of every licensed inspector and broker in Texas.

Information About Brokerage Services

Sections 1101.557, 1101.558, 1101.559, 1101.560, and 1101.561 of the license law addresses agency relationships between licensees and the public. One provision requires that a licensee, at the first substantive discussion, provide the prospect with the Information About Brokerage Services form. A *substantive discussion* is defined as the first discussion at which substantive information about a particular property or a prospect's ability to buy or lease occurs. The notice must be printed in a font no smaller than 10-point type.

■ NON-REALTY ITEMS

If the parties insist upon adding some additional items of personal property (non-realty items) that are to stay with the property (that are not already listed in 2B or 2C), attach TREC's Non-Realty Items Addendum to the contract.

■ TEXAS REAL ESTATE CONSUMER NOTICE CONCERNING HAZARDS OR DEFICIENCIES

The Texas Real Estate Consumer Notice Concerning Hazards or Deficiencies is an optional form that can be used to help the buyer understand the reason for the inspector reporting many items that were acceptable when the home was built (and are still functioning), but have been grandfathered as the codes changed. These are items the buyer needs to be aware of and, at sometime in the future, may want to upgrade. The buyer is free to try to negotiate for the seller to fix or replace some of the items, but the seller has no obligation to do so. The licensee may want to give the buyer the form when they start discussing the need for a home inspection. It may help the buyer to understand that the purpose of the inspection is for their information and they cannot assume the seller will fix anything. If there is a major item discovered and the seller will not negotiate the repair, the buyer may elect to terminate under their option to terminate if they have one.

■ ADDENDUM FOR PROPERTY IN A PROPANE GAS SYSTEM SERVICE AREA

Section 141.001 of the Texas Utilities Code defines propane gas system as "one or more propane storage containers, equipment, and facilities connected to a contiguous piping system through which propane gas is supplied by a distribution system retailer to at least 10 customers."

When someone purchases property located in a propane gas system service area, they might be required to pay a fee before they can receive propane gas service. Sometimes there is a period required to construct lines or other facilities necessary to provide propane gas service to that property.

New legislation requires the seller to notify the buyer if the property is in the propane gas system service area prior to the buyer signing the contract.

Licensees need to advise buyers to determine if the property is in a propane gas system service area and contact the distribution system retailer to determine the fee they will be required to pay and the period, if any, that is required to provide propane gas service to the property.

■ SUMMARY

TREC promulgates 15 addenda to address situations that aren't covered (or aren't covered in enough detail) in the promulgated contracts. Licensees need to be familiar with the situations that warrant the use of addenda and how to correctly fill them out. All licensees are required to use the TREC-promulgated addenda when one exists for that situation.

TREC has created and approved a number of addenda and other notices for use by licensees but they are not mandatory. These are the TREC forms with the prefix "OP" (e.g., TREC OP-L, Lead-Based Paint Addendum).

■ CONTRACT WORKSHOP

1. How does the broker satisfy the statutory requirement that the broker advise a buyer that the buyer should have an abstract of title examined by an attorney, or receive a policy of title insurance, when the broker is using a TREC contract form? What if a TREC form is not used?
2. If a Back-Up Contract is negotiated with an option period of ten days, with an original effective date of September 5, and an amended effective date of September 16, when does the option period end?
3. If the seller wants to be able to accept back up offers on his property, is it necessary to add that to special provisions in paragraph 11 of the TREC Contract?

■ WHICH FORM DO I USE?

For each scenario in the numbered list below, indicate which form, if any, should be used. Letters can be used more than once.

a. Seller's Temporary Residential Lease (*see* Chapter 5)
b. Addendum for Sale of Other Property By Buyer
c. No addendum; add to Special Provisions (paragraph 11; *see* Chapter 5)
d. Addendum for Back-Up Contract
e. No addendum needed; included in the contract
f. Buyer's Temporary Residential Lease (*see* Chapter 5)
g. Seller Financing Addendum (*see* Chapter 3)
h. Addendum for Release of Liability on Assumed Loan and/or Restoration of Seller's VA Entitlement
i. Environmental Assessment, Threatened or Endangered Species, and Wetlands Addendum (*see* Chapter 4)
j. Lead Based Paint Addendum (Addendum for Seller's Disclosure of Information on Lead-Based Paint and Lead-Based Paint Hazards as Required by Federal Law; *see* Chapter 4)
k. Notice of Buyer's Termination of Contract
l. Amendment (*see* Chapter 5)

1. _____ The buyer you are working with wants an abstract, rather than a title policy, on the acreage he is going to buy.

2. _____ The buyer wants to make an offer contingent upon the seller agreeing to allow the buyer to move in two weeks prior to closing.

3. _____ The buyer wants the seller to reimburse her for a Residential Service Policy.

4. _____ The buyer wants his offer to be contingent upon his home, which is already under contract, closing as scheduled.

5. _____ The seller is going to carry a second lien for a portion of her equity.

6. _____ The buyer wants to have the property inspected and have the right to just walk away from the contract.

7. _____ The seller has accepted a contingency offer on her property. She has received another offer and would like to negotiate the second offer, but does not want to take a chance on being obligated to sell to two different parties.

8. _____ The buyer and seller have agreed that they want to mediate if a dispute arises related to the contract that cannot be solved by negotiations.

9. _____ The seller is agreeable to the offer if the buyer will allow him to remain in the property for three days after closing.

10. _____ The buyer wants to exercise her right to terminate under paragraph 23.

11. _____ The property was built prior to 1978.

12. _____ A seller's home is being sold and his VA loan is being assumed. The seller hopes to have his VA entitlement restored.

13. _____ A prospective buyer is concerned that part of the property she is interested in may be wetlands.

14. _____ The buyer's contract gives him the right to terminate. After inspections, he decides that he still wants to buy the property, but at a reduced price.

■ TRUE/FALSE QUIZ

What do you remember about the TREC forms? Try to do the following without looking at the forms.

1. A contract is subject to financing. The loan is turned down by the lender because the property did NOT appraise for enough money. The buyer will be in default if the option period has already expired.
   a. True
   b. False

2. The sales price is $100,000. The buyer is making a first lien mortgage for $80,000, and the seller is carrying a second lien for $10,000. The amount in paragraph 3B should be $80,000.
   a. True
   b. False

3. Paragraph 7B(2) of the Residential Sales Contract is checked, and three days are entered in the blank. The Seller Disclosure is delivered on time. Two days later, the buyer sees another home he likes better. The buyer is free to terminate this contract even though he did NOT pay for an option to terminate.
   a. True
   b. False

4. If the buyer agrees to deliver a credit report to the seller, according to Paragraph A of the TREC Seller Financing Addendum, the cost of the report will be the buyer's expense.
   a. True
   b. False

5. If a buyer does *NOT* deposit the earnest money as agreed in the TREC One to Four Family Residential Contract (Resale), the buyer will be in default.
   a. True
   b. False

6. The title company furnishes copies of the restrictive covenants to the buyer at the seller's expense.
   a. True
   b. False

7. A buyer receives the survey and discovers a utility easement created by the dedication deed and plat of the subdivision. The buyer discovers that the easement is in an area that will prevent the addition of a swimming pool. If nothing has been added to the TREC One to Four Family Residential Contract (Resale), the buyer has the right to terminate the contract if she objects within the proper time frame.
   a. True
   b. False

8. Paragraph 7G of the TREC One to Four Family Residential Contract (Resale) cautions the buyer to use an addendum regarding environmental issues if he is concerned about those matters.
   a. True
   b. False

9. If a seller wants to continue to show her property for back-up offers, it is necessary to add that information to paragraph 11 of the TREC One to Four Family Residential Contract (Resale).
   a. True
   b. False

10. A seller who is a lender that has foreclosed on the property is exempt from obligation to give the Seller's Disclosure Notice. No boxes will be checked under paragraph 7B.
    a. True
    b. False

11. If the buyer and seller agree that the seller will have the foundation repaired and the buyer wants the warranty for that work transferred to him, the transfer will be at the buyer's expense according to the TREC One to Four Family Residential Contract (Resale).
    a. True
    b. False

12. If a property has mandatory membership in an owners association, it is necessary to use the TREC Addendum for Property Subject to Mandatory Membership in an Owners' Association and to list that Addendum in paragraph 11.
    a. True
    b. False

13. The TREC One to Four Family Residential Contract (Resale) has a provision that makes any party that fails or refuses to sign a release of escrow liable to the other party for liquidated damages in the amount of three times the amount of the earnest money.
    a. True
    b. False

14. When using the TREC One to Four Family Residential Contract (Resale), if you are acting as an intermediary, it is necessary for you to add the Buyer's Representation Agreement and add it in paragraph 22.
    a. True
    b. False

15. If no changes are made to the TREC One to Four Family Residential Contract (Resale), the seller will furnish the buyer a Special Warranty Deed at the time of closing.
    a. True
    b. False

16. If any sales expense exceeds the amount agreed to by a party in the TREC One to Four Family Residential Contract (Resale), that party may terminate the contract unless the other party agrees to pay the excess.
    a. True
    b. False

17. According to the TREC One to Four Family Residential Contract (Resale), if a PMI premium is due, it is a negotiable item between the buyer and seller.
    a. True
    b. False

18. If a property is damaged by fire, after it has been put under contract, and the seller is unable to repair the damage by the closing date, one of the buyer's options, according to the TREC One to Four Family Residential Contract (Resale), is to accept the property in its damaged condition and accept an assignment of the insurance proceeds.
    a. True
    b. False

19. The Seller's Disclosure Notice should be attached to the contract and listed in paragraph 22.
    a. True
    b. False

20. According to paragraph 18 of the TREC One to Four Family Residential Contract (Resale), if the buyer and seller mutually agree to terminate the contract and the seller agrees to release the earnest money to the buyer, the title company must refund all of the earnest money to the buyer.
    a. True
    b. False

CHAPTER 7 QUIZ

1. An agent is selling a new home and is using the builder-required contract form. How can the agent make sure the buyer receives the required notice that the buyer should have the abstract examined by an attorney or obtain a policy of title insurance?
   a. It will be in the builder contract.
   b. Use TREC form OP-C Notice to Prospective Buyer.
   c. New homes are exempt from the requirement.
   d. It will be in the listing agreement.

2. Which of the following addenda contains the words *time is of the essence*?
   a. Addendum for Sale of Other Property by Buyer
   b. Addendum for Reservation of Oil, Gas, and Other Minerals
   c. Addendum for Release of Liability on Assumed Loan and/or Restoration of Seller's VA Entitlement
   d. Addendum for Coastal Area Property

3. Who completes the promulgated resale certificate?
   a. Seller
   b. Homeowners association
   c. Buyer
   d. Listing agent

4. If a transaction is contingent upon the sale of buyer 1's property and the seller notifies buyer 1 that the seller has accepted a back-up offer, buyer 1 must
   a. waive the contingency on or before the date they have agreed upon in the Sale of Other Property Addendum.
   b. pay the additional earnest money agreed to in the Sale of Other Property Addendum.
   c. waive all negotiations of repairs.
   d. both a. and b.

5. A back-up contract was executed on August 9. The parties agreed to a 12-day option period. On August 15, the seller notified the buyer that the first contract had terminated. When does the buyer's option period end?
   a. At 5:00 pm on August 27
   b. At noon on August 21
   c. At noon on August 27
   d. At 5:00 pm on August 21

6. A back-up contract was executed on July 1. The buyer is willing to be in back-up position until July 16 and see if the first contract will terminate. What are the back-up buyer's responsibilities while they are in back-up position?
   a. Pay any earnest money agreed to in the back-up contract
   b. Make loan application with a lender
   c. Pay any option money agreed to in the back-up contract
   d. Both a. and c.

7. The Addendum for Coastal Area Property and the Addendum for Property Located Seaward of the Gulf Intracoastal Waterway contain the notices required by the
   a. Texas Real Estate Commission.
   b. Texas Real Estate License Act.
   c. Texas Natural Resources Code.
   d. One to Four Family Residential Contract.

8. Which form should be used when a seller wants to sell his property for less than what is owed on the property?
   a. Addendum for Release of Liability on Assumed Loan and/or Restoration of Seller's VA Entitlement
   b. Short Sale Addendum
   c. Notice of Buyer's Termination of Contract
   d. Addendum for Sale of Other Property By Buyer

9. A buyer decides to exercise her right to terminate under the option period. What is the proper process?
    a. Execute a Notice of Termination of Contract
    b. Deliver the Notice of Termination to the Title Company
    c. Deliver the Notice of Termination of Contract to the seller according to the instructions in paragraph 21 of the contract
    d. Both a. and c.

10. Who is required to execute the Notice of Termination of Contract?
    a. Only the buyer
    b. Only the seller
    c. Both the buyer and the seller
    d. The buyer, the seller, and both agents

CHAPTER

Other Real Estate Matters

■ **LEARNING OBJECTIVES**   *When you have completed this chapter, you will be able to*

- ■ **describe** current forms of fraud and how it affects licensees and the public;
- ■ **identify** on which forms brokers' fees are agreed upon;
- ■ **identify** the protected classes under the fair housing laws in Texas;
- ■ **list** disclosures that are required, permitted, and prohibited; and
- ■ **describe** HUD's occupancy standards.

■ KEY TERMS

Fair Housing Act
fraud

multiple listing service
(MLS)

■ REAL ESTATE FRAUD

Unfortunately, real estate **fraud** is growing and is a losing proposition. When these losses take place, they damage everyone. Consumers end up paying the price for this loss.

The results of fraud are as varied as the different types of fraud. It can result in inflated appraisals and property values, bogus documents recorded in public records, monetary losses and frustration for victims, penalties for perpetrators, damaged reputations, and new laws. Licensees need to be aware of fraud in its different forms to prevent damages to themselves and their brokers, clients, customers, and the public, and to keep from participating in fraud themselves, intentional or not.

Fraud Perpetrated by Buyers or Sellers

Fraud is everywhere and committed by many different individuals. It evolves constantly in response to increased scrutiny and laws, and as new methods prove to be profitable (at least in the short run). Some current forms are included here, but an important takeaway for all licensees is to pay attention, listen to your instincts (if it doesn't sound right, it's probably not; if it sounds too good to be true, it probably is), and consult your broker or firm's attorney if you have any concerns.

Flipping   When a property is purchased and then quickly resells at a value that is artificially inflated by false appraisals, loan fraud has taken place. Often, the first buyer is reselling the property to someone that is participating in the fraudulent activity. For example, if the first buyer purchases a home for $400,000 (which is the actual value) and then resells it at $600,000 with a phony appraisal to a straw (phony) buyer, the first buyer and straw buyer might both pocket $100,000. No payments are made on the $600,000 loan, and upon foreclosure, the lender discovers that the property is only worth $400,000. The lender takes the loss and their costs increase.

Buyer Rebates   Anything during the transaction that causes money to go back to the buyer, either at or after closing, without the knowledge of the lender, is illegal. Sometimes the money comes from the seller, sometimes from the real estate agent or the mortgage loan broker, and sometimes through a third-party vendor. It is essential that the lender know exactly how much money for down payment and/or closing costs are being paid from the buyer's own funds. Anything being paid by any other party in the transaction must be disclosed in the contract and on the closing documents.

One of the common forms of rebates happens when the contract calls for money to be paid to a certain vendor for improvements to be made after closing. For example, $20,000 is to be paid by the seller to ABC Home Improvements for future improvements. ABC Home Improvements is actually owned by a friend of the buyer, and after closing, the friend and the buyer split the $20,000. No improvements are made and no mortgage payments are made. Upon foreclosure, the lender finds that the property is worth less than the loan amount.

Red Flags

Almost everyone involved in a real estate transaction could be involved in fraud: the agents, the mortgage broker, the appraiser, the title company, et cetera. The lender is usually the victim.

Licensees can learn to spot fraud. The following is a list of some red flags that might indicate fraudulent activity in a real estate transaction:

- Inflated price and/or appraisal
- Licensee is frequently asked to remove the property from the **multiple listing service (MLS)** (which is a violation of MLS rules) or asked to increase the price in the MLS

- False financial statements by the buyer
- Contract calling for future improvements
- High fees to the mortgage broker, real estate broker, or both
- No fee for a title policy on the closing documents
- A title company the licensee has never heard of before
- Last-minute amendments to the contract, increasing the sales price

Risk Management

When licensees suspect fraud, they should do the following to protect themselves and the parties to the transaction:

- Document everything
- Disclose everything to the lender (representing the buyer does not include helping the buyer cheat the lender)
- Verify the accuracy of items on the closing documents
- Withdraw from a transaction that appears to be fraudulent and tell the seller to seek legal advice if the seller intends to continue with the transaction

Fraud Perpetrated by Licensees

Deceptive Trade Practices—Consumer Protection Act   One very important consideration in fraud that involves licensees is the Deceptive Trade Practices—Consumer Protection Act.

The Texas Deceptive Trade Practices—Consumer Protection Act (DTPA) is Chapter 17, Subchapter E of the Business and Commerce Code. This act declares, among other things, that "false, misleading or deceptive acts or practices" in the advertising, offering for sale, selling, or leasing of any real or personal property are unlawful. As set forth in the act, false, misleading, or deceptive acts or practices are included in a "laundry list" of 27 items; some of them are as follows:

- Representing that something is new or original when it is not, or that it is of a particular quality when it is not
- Advertising property with no intention of selling the property as advertised
- Making false statements of fact concerning the reasons for a price reduction
- Misrepresenting the authority of an agent to negotiate the final terms of a sales contract
- Representing that a warranty guarantees or confers rights or remedies not included
- Representing that work has been done on real or personal property when the work has not been done

In 2011, the Texas Legislature sought to reduce frivolous lawsuits against real estate brokers and salespersons by providing that the DTPA does not apply to claims arising from an act or omission by a broker or salesperson, with certain exceptions (S.B. 1353, 2011). The three circumstances under which the DTPA does apply to the actions of real estate agents are

- "an express misrepresentation of a material fact that cannot be characterized as advice, judgment, or opinion;"
- a failure to disclose information concerning goods or services that was known at the time of the transaction if the failure to disclose such

information was intended to induce the consumer into a transaction which the consumer would not have entered had the information been disclosed; or
- "an unconscionable action or course of action that cannot be characterized as advice, judgment, or opinion."

In a DTPA suit, the consumer must prove that the deceptive act was the producing cause of damages. The suit must be commenced within two years after a false, misleading, or deceptive act or practice occurred—or within two years after the consumer discovered, or should have discovered, the deceptive act or practice. With the exception of residential property, the DTPA does not apply to transactions that exceed $100,000 where there is a written contract and the consumer is represented by legal counsel.

By statute, consumers may waive their rights to bring a suit under the DTPA. However, court opinions consistently uphold that "any waiver by a consumer of the provisions of the subchapter is contrary to public policy and is unenforceable and void." Therefore, all of the following strict requirements must be met for the waiver to be valid and enforceable:

- The waiver must be in writing and signed by the consumer.
- The consumer must not be in a significantly disparate bargaining position.
- The consumer must be represented by legal counsel (not referred by the defendant or an agent of the defendant) in seeking or acquiring the goods or services.
- The waiver must be conspicuous and in boldface type at least 10 points in size.
- The waiver must be in substantially the promulgated form under the heading "Waiver of Consumer Rights."

Either party to a lawsuit filed under the DTPA may file a motion to compel mediation of the dispute. Defenses to the DTPA include (1) a reasonable offer of settlement within specified time limits, (2) written notice to the consumer prior to consummation of the sale that the broker is relying on written information prepared by others, and (3) the impossibility of the broker's knowing that the information was false or inaccurate. The act also permits recovery of court costs and attorneys' fees if the lawsuit was ruled frivolous or harassing.

Recovery under the DTPA is limited to economic damages—costs of repair and replacement. However, if the defendant is found to have committed the act knowingly, then damages for mental anguish may also be awarded (and in some cases, up to three times the amount of economic damages). If the defendant is found to have committed the act intentionally, then the economic and mental anguish damages may be trebled. In addition to consumer compensation, the DTPA allows for civil penalties of up to $20,000 per violation, with an additional penalty of up to $250,000 for deceptive acts or practices that target the elderly. Note that an errors and omissions insurance policy purchased by a broker will not cover fraud or intentional violations of the DTPA. (St. Paul Insurance Company v. Bonded Realty, Inc. 583 S.W.2d 619 [Tex. 1979] p. 141.)

Under Section 1101.805 of the License Act, parties to a contract and licensees are protected from liability for misrepresentation or concealment of material facts by each other or by a subagent unless the party or licensee knew of the falsity or concealment. A defendant who is only marginally at fault in a claim will be liable to the consumer for that defendant's percentage of responsibility. In addition to proportionate responsibility, a defendant may be held jointly and separately responsible for all damages recoverable by the claimant if (a) the defendant's percentage of responsibility is greater than 50% or (b) the defendant, with specific intent to do harm to others, acted with another person to engage in a felony of the third degree or higher—including forgery, misapplication of fiduciary property, or securing execution of a document by deception. However, proportional responsibility laws do not diminish the broker's liability for the acts of the broker's salespersons, for whom the broker is still fully responsible.

Loss of License

TRELA Sec. 1101.652 provides for the suspension or revocation of a real estate license by the Texas Real Estate Commission for various offenses. Sec. 1101.652(a)(1) states

> (a) The commission may suspend or revoke a license issued under this chapter or take other disciplinary action authorized by this chapter if the license holder:
> (1) enters a plea of guilty or nolo contendere to or is convicted of a felony or a criminal offense involving fraud, and the time for appeal has elapsed or the judgment or conviction has been affirmed on appeal, without regard to an order granting community supervision that suspends the imposition of the sentence.

Depending on the severity of the fraud, suspension or loss of license could be the least of a licensee's concerns.

■ BROKERS' FEES

As discussed in Chapter 4, most of the TREC contract forms do not discuss the broker's commission. Paragraph 8 of the contract reads, "All obligations of the parties for payment of brokers' fees are contained in separate written agreements."

So where are these separate written agreements?

- The listing agreement is an agreement between seller and broker.
- The buyer's representation agreement is an agreement between buyer and broker.
- An agreement between brokers is either a written agreement or through the MLS system.

The agreement between brokers is referred to on the last page of the sales contract: "Listing Broker has agreed to pay Other Broker _____ of the total sales price when the Listing Broker's fee is received. Escrow agent is authorized and directed to pay other Broker from Listing Broker's fee at closing."

This is not the agreement between brokers; it only affirms what the agreement is. If the property is in MLS, the amount in this blank should be the same as the sub agency compensation (SAC) or buyer agency compensation (BAC) in MLS.

The listing agreement usually has a clause saying the seller will pay a commission to the listing broker. This commission usually includes the amount the listing broker is going to earn for their service plus an amount the listing broker intends to share with the broker that brings a buyer.

The buyer's representation agreement usually has a clause saying the buyer will pay a commission to the selling broker. Frequently, it says that the selling broker will try to collect the commission first from the seller or the seller's agents, and only if they are unable to collect it from the seller or their agents does the buyer owe any amount. For example, if the buyer's representation agreement says that the buyer's broker will receive 3.5% and the MLS printout says the listing broker is offering the selling broker 3.5%, the buyer would owe nothing. In this case, the agreement between brokers is through MLS. When a listing broker enters a property in MLS and enters an amount under SAC or BAC that is an offer to selling agents to participate in the sale and receive compensation of a certain amount.

When a selling agent shows the property and writes an offer, the listing broker's offer of compensation has been accepted. This agreement can't be changed simply by entering a different amount in the final page of the contract.

If the property is not in MLS, even if the listing broker is a member of MLS, there is no offer of compensation. A buyer's agent should get an agreement between brokers signed before showing the property to be clear on the offer. Remember, the Statute of Frauds says anything regarding real estate must be in writing to be enforceable.

FAIR HOUSING LAWS

The Fair Housing Act

The Fair Housing Act covers most housing. In some circumstances, the act exempts owner-occupied buildings with no more than four units, single-family housing sold or rented without the use of a broker, and housing operated by organizations and private clubs that limit occupancy to members. However, an owner who is exempt from the Fair Housing Act may still be liable for racial discrimination under the Civil Rights Act of 1866. There are no exceptions under that act.

In the sale and rental of housing, no one may take any of the following actions based on an applicant's race, color, national origin, religion, sex, familial status, or disability:

- Refuse to rent or sell housing
- Refuse to negotiate for housing
- Make housing unavailable
- Set different terms, conditions, or privileges for sale or rental of a dwelling
- Provide different housing services or facilities
- Falsely deny that housing is available for inspection, sale, or rental
- For profit, persuade owners to sell or rent (blockbusting)
- Deny anyone access to or membership in a facility or service (such as a multiple listing service) related to the sale or rental of housing

Local and state fair housing laws and professional organizations can add to the federal law's list of protected classes. For instance, in its Code of Ethics, the National Association of REALTORS® has added sexual orientation as a protected class. In their real estate practice, all REALTORS® must honor sexual orientation as a protected class in addition to the seven classes protected under the federal law. In addition to the protected groups in federal and Texas fair housing laws, TRELA §1101.652(b)(32) and TREC Rule §531.19(a)(6) add ancestry as an additional category to the protected classes.

Protections for Individuals with Disabilities

A *disability* is a physical or mental impairment. It is unlawful to discriminate against prospective buyers or tenants on the basis of disability. The term includes those having a history of, or being regarded as having, an impairment that substantially limits one or more major life activities. Persons who have AIDS are protected by the fair housing laws under this classification.

The federal Fair Housing Act's protection of people with disabilities does not include those who are current users of illegal or controlled substances. Individuals who have been convicted of the illegal manufacture or distribution of a controlled substance are also not protected under this law. However, the law does prohibit discrimination against those who are participating in addiction recovery programs. For instance, a landlord could lawfully discriminate against a cocaine addict but not against a member of Alcoholics Anonymous.

A landlord may not do the following:

■ Refuse to let a person with disabilities make reasonable modifications to dwellings or common use areas, at the person's expense, if the modifications are necessary for the person to use the housing. Where reasonable, the landlord may permit changes only if the person agrees to restore the property to its original condition upon move-out.
■ Refuse to make reasonable accommodations in rules, policies, practices or services if necessary for a person with disabilities to use the housing

Here are a few examples:

■ A building with a "no pets" policy must allow a visually impaired tenant to keep a guide dog.
■ An apartment complex that offers tenants ample, unassigned parking must honor a request from a mobility-impaired tenant for a reserved space near her apartment if necessary to assure that she can have access to her apartment.

Housing need not be made available to a person who is a direct threat to the health or safety of others or who currently uses illegal drugs.

Housing Opportunities for Families

Unless a building or community qualifies as housing for older persons, it may not discriminate based on familial status. That is, it may not discriminate against families in which one or more children under the age of 18 live with

- a parent,
- a person who has legal custody of the child or children, or
- the designee of the parent or legal custodian, with the parent or custodian's written permission.

Familial status protection also applies to pregnant women and anyone securing legal custody of a child under the age of 18.

Housing for older persons is exempt from the prohibition against familial status discrimination if any of the following:

- The HUD Secretary has determined that it is specifically designed for and occupied by elderly persons under a federal, state, or local program.
- It is occupied solely by persons age 62 or older.
- It is occupied by at least one person 55 years of age or older per unit (where 80% of the units are occupied by individuals age 55 or older).
- It adheres to a policy that demonstrates an intent to house persons age 55 or older.

■ OTHER DISCLOSURES

Required

Many disclosures are required when selling property. Everything the sellers or agents know about the condition of the property must be disclosed to potential buyers. Any information or reports regarding the roof, structure, electrical, plumbing, drainage, et cetera, must be shared with the buyer to prevent future lawsuits. The Seller's Disclosure Notice signed by the buyer is the seller's proof of disclosure. Paragraph 6E (1-9) discloses many things to the buyer that are required by law. Anytime you are using a form other than a TREC form you have to be aware to give those required notices by a different method.

Permitted

There are a few disclosures that are not required but are permitted. For example, disclosing a suicide that took place in a property is not required but permitted if the seller chooses to disclose it. Another example is the disclosure of registered sex offenders in the neighborhood. It is not required. The disclosure is permitted, but it is often best to just provide the resources to buyers to investigate for themselves. In Texas, sex offender information may be found at the Texas Department of Public Safety website, www.dps.texas.gov.

Prohibited

A good business practice is to never disclose anything about the most stringent fair housing protected classes (e.g., if local law adds additional protected classes, use that as the basis).

HIV and AIDS are included in the protected class of disability under the Fair Housing Act. The disclosure that a previous or current occupant has AIDS or an HIV-related illness is not required. Additionally, HUD, NAR, and the Canons of Professional Ethics in TRELA advise against disclosure, inquiry, or response regarding this issue.

The Texas Real Estate License Act reads:

> *Notwithstanding Subsection (b) of this section, a person is not subject to civil liability or criminal prosecution because the person did not inquire about, make a disclosure related to, or release information related to whether a previous or current occupant of real property had, may have had, has or may have AIDS, HIV related illnesses or HIV infection as defined by the Center for Disease Control of the U.S. Public Health Service.*

■ OCCUPANCY STANDARDS

Neither the Fair Housing Act nor HUD has a particular rule regarding occupancy. Both allow for housing providers to comply with reasonable local, state, and federal occupancy restrictions. In some cases, housing providers have been permitted to develop and implement reasonable occupancy restrictions on their own.

The primary intention of HUD is to make sure the occupancy standards are not so strict as to eliminate the protection of families with children. For example, an apartment building that limits one bedroom apartments to only one person would probably not be acceptable because the one person would certainly be an adult, eliminating children.

In a statement of policy, effective December 18, 1998, HUD stated that two people per bedroom was a reasonable standard (and the age of the two people is not a consideration). They further clarified that when considering a complaint, they would consider if any policy was so strict it was making it difficult for families to find housing.

Using that information, we can conclude that HUD would probably agree that a four bedroom home would be available to a single parent and seven children. Property managers need to make sure their owners (landlords) are aware of the fair housing laws.

■ SUMMARY

Real estate fraud continues to be on the rise and takes various forms. Licensees who suspect fraud in a real estate transaction should document the issues, disclose information to pertinent parties as necessary, and withdraw from fraudulent transactions.

Broker's commission is discussed in written agreements separate from the TREC contract forms: the listing agreement, the buyer's representation agreement, or an agreement between brokers (either a written agreement or through the MLS).

The Fair Housing Act is a federal law that prohibits discrimination in housing based on race, color, religion, sex, disability, familial status, and national origin. Local and state laws can add to the federal law's list of protected classes.

CHAPTER 8 QUIZ

1. Red flags that a party may be making an offer that will be involved in real estate fraud include
   a. an offer calling for future improvements.
   b. an inflated sales price.
   c. a request to remove the property from MLS.
   d. all of these.

2. If you believe a transaction is involved in illegal activity, you should
   a. notify your broker.
   b. withdraw from the transaction.
   c. tell the seller to seek legal advice if they plan to continue with the transaction.
   d. all of these.

3. Contractual agreements between brokers may be defined in
   a. written agreements signed by both brokers.
   b. the MLS.
   c. the sales contract.
   d. both a. and b.

4. An owner might be exempt from the provisions of the Fair Housing Act if the owner is attempting to rent out
   a. one of the units in the duplex in which she lives.
   b. an apartment in a five-unit complex that is across the street from her house.
   c. an apartment in a three-unit complex using the assistance of a licensee.
   d. an apartment in a five-unit complex in which her brother lives.

5. Familial status in the Fair Housing Act protects
   a. families with children under the age of 18.
   b. all families.
   c. pregnant women.
   d. both a. and c.

6. Real estate fraud is harmful to
   a. lenders.
   b. consumers.
   c. buyers.
   d. everyone.

7. If anyone is helping the buyer with the down payment or closing cost,
   a. it must be disclosed to the title company.
   b. it is not necessary to disclose it.
   c. it must be disclosed to the lender on the contract and on the closing documents.
   d. it must be disclosed to the seller.

8. The agreement between the brokers regarding the amount to be paid by the listing broker to the selling broker is a contractual agreement contained in the
   a. Listing Agreement.
   b. Agreement between Brokers (frequently in MLS).
   c. Sales Contract.
   d. Buyer/Tenant Representation Agreement.

9. Which of the following is NOT a protected class under the Federal Fair Housing Act?
   a. Age
   b. Race
   c. Familial status
   d. Religion

10. The National Association of REALTORS® recently added _____ as a protected class under the NAR Code of Ethics.
    a. national origin
    b. color
    c. smokers
    d. sexual orientation

CHAPTER 9

Practice Makes Perfect

■ **LEARNING OBJECTIVES**   *When you have completed this chapter, you will be able to*

- **complete** a sample transaction using these forms:
  — One to Four Family Residential Contract
  — Lead-Based Paint Addendum
  — Third Party Financing Addendum
- **complete** a sample transaction using these forms:
  — One to Four Family Residential Contract
  — Environmental Assessment, Threatened or Endangered Species, and Wetlands Addendum
  — Seller Financing Addendum
- **complete** a sample transaction using
  — Residential Condominium Contract (Resale)
  — Loan Assumption Addendum
  — Addendum for Back-up Contract
  — Addendum for Coastal Area Property
  — Addendum for Property Located Seaward of the Gulf Intracoastal Waterway
  — Addendum for Release of Liability on Assumed Loan and/or Restoration of Seller's VA Entitlement

Refer to Texas Promulgated Forms Supplement for the forms needed for these transactions.

■ TRANSACTION: FLEMING TO DONALDSON

Troy Donaldson and his wife, Donna, have found a home they want to make an offer on. Their current home at 1320 New Century Drive in Houston is a rental, and they are anxious to become homeowners. Because they believe their income can only increase, they have decided to finance the property on an adjustable rate mortgage. They can get an adjustable rate mortgage, fixed for one year, at 5% on conventional financing. The lender has told them the interest rate on the loan cannot adjust for more than 2% a year or 5% over the life of the loan. There is a 1% origination fee but no discount points.

Larry and Marcia Fleming have owned the home the Donaldson's would like to purchase since it was built in 1975. It is in good repair except for the four fogged windows in the kitchen. The property is located at 3430 Old Master Drive in Houston, Texas 77056 and is owner occupied.

The Donaldsons decide to offer $325,000 for the property. They will be putting 10% down. The loan will include PMI. They will put up $3,500 as earnest money and a $1,500 option fee will be paid to the seller. They have received and reviewed the Seller's Disclosure. They want 15 days to investigate everything about the property and be able to terminate if they decide to do so. They want the $1,500 to be credited to the sales price at the time of closing.

The Donaldsons want the four fogged windows in the kitchen to be repaired, and they want to be sure they will be able to put in a pool after closing, and that they will be able to park their RV in the driveway. They are going to ask the seller to pay for the title policy, but they are willing to pay for a new survey at their expense. They do not feel they need the survey amendment to the title policy.

The buyers do want a residential service contract and are going to ask the sellers to reimburse them $425.

The listing agent is Tom Price with Wonderful Properties at 1213 Sellmore Street in Houston, Texas 77056, and you are the selling agent and are with I Sell More Properties at 2033 Winston Avenue, Corsicanna, Texas 75308. You are representing the buyers.

Tom's telephone number is 713-276-4799, fax 713-298-2245 and email address is tomprice@gmail.com.

Both the parties travel, so they want any notices to be sent to their agents.

Tom has a 5% listing with the Flemings. Tom is offering 4% in BAC in the MLS system.

Closing will be at the end of next month, and possession will be at closing and funding. The parties agree they would want to mediate if the situation warrants it.

The closer will be Larry Spence at ABC Title Company at 1219 Goldrich Street, Houston, TX 77057. Larry's telephone number is 713-278-4901, fax is 713-278-4900, and email address is Larryspence@abctitle.com.

Use this information to complete the offer.

■ TRANSACTION: JOHNSON TO SWANSON

Tim J. Swanson and his wife, Sarah J. Swanson, will purchase a second home. It is known as Lot 6, Block 8 of the Terrace Addition of Waco, McLennan County, Texas 76710. They are willing to pay $73,500 for it if the owner, Samuel A. Johnson, a bachelor, will owner finance $25,000 for five years at 5% annual interest. The buyers will pay monthly interest only until maturity when the principal balance is due. They agree to a due-on-sale clause in the deed of trust and will provide paid tax receipts by February 1 of each year the loan is outstanding.

The Swansons request a title policy issued by Secure Title Company and a new survey showing no encroachments or easements other than the 10-foot utility easement at the rear of the lot. The buyers want ten days for objections to survey and title commitment. The seller will pay for the title policy. The Swansons want to make certain that cable TV services are available. They have received the Seller's Disclosure Notice and buy a 10-day option to terminate for $150 to have the opportunity to thoroughly evaluate the property. The option fee will not be credited to the sales price at closing. Possession will be granted at closing and funding.

The closer for Secure Title Company will be Tina Frost. Secure's office address is 1010 Westway, Waco, TX 76710. Tina's telephone number is 817-694-1010, fax is 817-694-1011, and email address is tina@securetitle.com.

The property is not subject to a mandatory owners association assessment. It is listed with Smooth Sails Realty through whom the buyers purchase it without representation. They will close on or before May 27, which is within 15 days of the effective date of the contract. The seller requests that the buyers furnish a current credit report within five days after the effective date of the contract as evidence of good credit.

The property is located at 15630 Paradise Avenue in Waco, Texas 76710. The buyers want deletion of the common title policy exclusion relating to discrepancies, conflicts, and shortages in area or boundary and are willing to pay the additional 5% policy premium required by the title company. Earnest money in the amount of $2,000 has been tendered. The seller will provide a new survey within ten days at the seller's expense. The survey will be acceptable to the title company. The purchasers want to have an environmental assessment performed to make certain that there is no contamination and that no toxic materials are present. This they will do within ten days after the effective date of the contract. The parties also agree to mediate any disputes that may arise.

The Swansons want any notices sent to Tim at 1450 Crestridge Ave, Dallas, TX. Tim's telephone number is 214-590-1410 and email address is timswanson@amazon.com. Mr. Johnson wants any notices sent to himself at the property address. His telephone number is 817-283-1498 and email address is samaj@yahoo.com.

Use this information to complete the offer.

■ TRANSACTION: KRAMER TO SWEENEY

Unit 623 of Building B of the condominium project known as Freedom Flats, Phase II, in Corpus Christi, Nueces County, Texas, is being sold to Brian C. Sweeney and spouse, Ellie T. Sweeney, by Paul M. Kramer and his wife, Sarah S. Kramer. The property is more commonly known as 1215 Market Street, Apartment 623. Ownership of the unit includes two parking spaces identified as numbers 1654 and 1658 in the adjoining parking garage. The zip code is 78411.

The Sweeneys currently live at 1410 Texas Avenue in Galveston, TX. Their telephone number is 734-812-9015. Brian's email address is brian@sweenycorp.com.

Paul and Sarah Kramer do not have an email address. Their telephone number is 815-915-4765 and their fax is 815-915-4766.

Prior to signing the agreement of purchase, the buyers received, reviewed, and accepted all of the condominium documents, as well as the Condominium Resale Certificate that was prepared and signed by the secretary of the owners association 20 days ago.

The buyers will pay $368,200 for the unit and assume the seller's existing conventional loan with an outstanding balance of $265,008. The loan is a portfolio loan held by Deep Pocket Mortgage Company, Inc. The buyers will apply for assumption approval within three days after the effective date of the contract. They will close within 30 days of the effective date of this contract, which will allow for closing on June 16. Possession will be at closing and funding. The current loan is at 4.5% and may be escalated to 5% upon assumption. If the loan balance is a few dollars more or less at closing, the cash payable at closing will be adjusted to compensate for any variance. The lender will charge a 1-point transfer fee, which will be paid by the buyers.

The buyers will pay for the owners' title policy. The buyers want 3 days to object after receiving the commitment. The buyers received the Seller's Disclosure Notice and accept the property in its present condition provided the seller, at seller's expense, shall replace the nonfunctioning garbage disposal and the broken faucet in the bathroom. Because the project was built in 1979, it is not subject to the HUD lead-based paint disclosure requirement. No repairs to any of the common elements are required. The buyers are not asking for a residential service contract.

The sellers have informed the buyers that the monthly principal, interest, taxes, and insurance (PITI) payment is $2,885 and the monthly maintenance fee is $236. The resale certificate furnished by the secretary of the owners association confirmed the amount of the maintenance fee. The buyers will pay any transfer or processing fee charged by the owners association.

The sellers will have the purchase agreement reviewed by Attorney Michael Holmes prior to signing the agreement. Mr. Holmes's office is at 1009 Baker Street, Corpus Christi and his email address is Michael.holmes@attorney.com.

The unit has been listed with Skyline Realty. You are the listing agent. Your listing company will pay the subagent, Downhome Realty, a selling fee equal to 3.25% of the selling price of the property. Candy Criss is the selling agent and is also the broker at Downhome Realty. Candy's telephone number is 815-914-2691 and her email address is cc@downhomerealty.biz.

A sum of $2,000 in earnest money is delivered to Buyer's Choice Title Company, who will issue an owners' policy at closing. The closing agent is Weldon Cresson. Weldon's telephone number is 815-915-5284, fax is 815-915-5285 and email address is weldon@buyerschoice.com. The title company is located at 104 3rd Avenue, Corpus Christi, TX.

The sellers will deliver a copy of the note and deed of trust to the buyers for review within three days after the effective date of the purchase agreement. The buyers also request that copies of every document they will be asked to sign at closing be delivered to them for review a minimum of 48 hours prior to closing.

The buyers will pay the seller a $250 option fee for a seven day option period with the fee being credited back to them at closing.

The sellers will permit the loan to be assumed only if they are released from liability and will not close if the lender refuses to release them. The buyers and the sellers will apply for the release within three days after the effective date of the contract. The sellers have agreed to pay a release fee not to exceed $200.

There is already an existing contract in place, dated May 5, between the sellers and a bachelor, Mason Wright. If the sellers notify the buyers on or before 5:00 pm on May 20 that the contract with Mr. Wright is terminated, this agreement is no longer subject to the contingency, and the effective date of this contract will be amended to be the date of termination of the previous contract.

Use this information to complete the offer.

Glossary

abstract (of title) A full summary of all recorded documents, recorded at the county courthouse, that may affect title to a given parcel of real estate; addressed in paragraph 6 of the TREC-promulgated contracts.

acceptance An expression of intent to be bound by the terms and conditions of an offer. To bind the agreement, the acceptance must be communicated to the person making the offer. An offer pertaining to real estate must be made in writing and accepted in writing.

accessory An item identified as part of the sale in paragraph 2 of the TREC-promulgated contract forms that does not meet the test of a fixture; defined in paragraph 2 of the TREC-promulgated contract forms.

acknowledgment A formal declaration, made by a person signing a document, to a duly authorized public official that the document was signed by the signor's own free will. Documents must be acknowledged to be admissible for public recording.

addendum An addition to a contract; the contract must reference the addendum, and the addendum must reference the contract; listed in paragraph 22 of the TREC-promulgated contracts.

addition Another name for a platted subdivision; identified in paragraph 2 of the TREC-promulgated contract forms.

after Later than; in the TREC-promulgated contract forms, the counting of days is from the day after the date of signing or execution and does not include the day the document is signed.

affidavit A Residential Real Property Affidavit promulgated by the Texas Department of Insurance (*see* paragraph 6C of the One to Four Family Residential Contract).

amendment A revision or change to a contract; the TREC contracts may be amended by using the TREC-promulgated amendment.

annex (annexation) To add or attach to a municipality. The possibility is addressed in paragraph 6E(5) of the TREC-promulgated contract forms.

arbitration An alternative, nonjudicial, dispute resolution approach that submits the dispute to a selected third party who renders a decision that may or may not be binding upon the parties.

assignment The transfer of one's legal rights to another party.

assessments For periods prior to closing, additional taxes, penalties, or interest.

assumption To take on personal liability for a legal obligation made by another person.

attorney-in-fact A legally competent and neutral party who is authorized by another to act in that individual's place as a fiduciary.

back-up contract A secondary contract; a contract in which the contracting parties recognize the existence of a superior contract between one of the parties and a third party; created by use of the TREC Addendum for Back-Up Contract.

baron sole An unmarried man.

bilateral contract A contractual agreement in which each party agrees to perform or forbear in exchange for the other party's promise to perform or forebear.

breach (of contract) Nonperformance of the legal terms of a valid contract.

broker One who is licensed by the state to serve as a special agent to a buyer or seller in a real estate transaction.

Broker-Lawyer Committee In Texas, a statutorily created group of six brokers, six lawyers, and one public member who draft and recommend forms for promulgation by the Real Estate Commission.

broker's fee The compensation (commission) charged by a broker for professional services rendered; addressed in paragraph 8 of the TREC-promulgated contracts.

business detail A point of agreement in a contract that does not define legal rights and remedies.

buyer's agent A broker who represents the interests of the buyer and acts as the buyer's special agent.

buyer's expenses Expenses payable by the buyer (*see* paragraph 12A(2) of the One to Four Family Residential Contract).

casualty loss A financial loss caused by physical damage to the improvements on a parcel of real estate; remedies for a casualty loss are identified in paragraph 14 of the TREC-promulgated contract forms.

chain of title A history of the succession of ownership of a parcel of land.

closing   The consummation of a real estate transaction when the seller (grantor) delivers title to the buyer (grantee) and the buyer delivers consideration to the seller.

closing costs   Expenses paid at closing in addition to the purchase price of the property; paragraph 12 of the TREC-promulgated contracts identifies who is responsible for paying various closing costs.

closing date   A date established by the contracting parties or within seven days after objections made under paragraph 6D have been cured or voided, whichever date is later (*see* paragraph 9A of the One to Four Family Residential Contract).

commitment   A commitment for title insurance (*see* paragraph 6B of the One to Four Family Residential Contract).

community property   A system of property ownership based on the theory that each spouse has an equal interest in the property acquired by the efforts of either spouse during marriage.

competent party   A party who has legal capacity to enter into a binding contract.

completed construction   For the purposes of TREC-promulgated forms, a new home that is finished and ready for move-in.

condominium documents   The enabling and governing documents that create and guide the operations of a condominium project. Chapter 82 of the Texas Property Code establishes the statutory requirements to create a condominium.

consideration   Something of value given by one party in exchange for something of value from another; money for a promise, money for money, a promise for a promise.

contingency   A contractual provision that requires completion of a defined act before the contract is binding; the buyer, for example, must be approved for a loan before the buyer is obligated to perform and close the transaction.

contract   A legally enforceable agreement between two parties to do (performance) or not to do (forbearance) a particular act.

contract for deed   A purchase agreement that provides for deferred delivery of the title to the buyer (vendee) after the seller (vendor) has received all of the deferred payments due to be paid as the full consideration tendered for the property; identified as Executory Contract for Conveyance in section 5.061 of the Texas Property Code.

conventional   Third party financing that is neither insured or guaranteed by an agency of government. Third party lending is addressed on the first page of the Third Party Financing Addendum.

cooperating broker   The broker who brings the buyer to the transaction who may be functioning as either a subagent of the listing broker or a buyer's agent.

counteroffer   An offer made in response to an unacceptable offer.

declaration   The recorded document that legally establishes a condominium.

deed restriction   A provision placed in deeds, usually by the developer of a subdivision, that controls future use of the property; also called a restrictive covenant.

default   *See* breach of contract.

disclosure   A revelation of known facts; the Texas Property Code requires sellers of previously occupied single-family residences to disclose material facts about the physical condition of the property.

dual agent   A broker who has received the informed consent of both the seller and the buyer to represent both of the parties in a real estate transaction under common law principles, rather than functioning as an intermediary as defined by statute.

earnest money   The initial and additional cash deposits tendered by the prospective buyer of real property to show good faith. Earnest money and additional earnest money are addressed in paragraph 5 of the TREC-promulgated contracts and in the TREC Addendum for Back-Up Contract.

effective date   The date on which the offeree accepts the offer and the offeror is notified of the acceptance. The Statute of Frauds requires that the offer and acceptance be in writing; the notification may be verbal. The TREC contract forms call for the broker to fill in the effective date.

endangered species   Certain fish, animal, and plant life that the federal government has determined to be in danger of extinction.

enforceable contract   An agreement that meets all of the legal requirements to create a binding contract.

entitlement   The portion of a VA-guaranteed loan that is guaranteed to the lender if the veteran defaults on the loan.

escrow   The act of putting money and documents in the care of a third, disinterested party until certain conditions are met. Paragraph 18 of the TREC-promulgated contracts addresses the responsibilities of the escrow agent.

Et ux   And wife

Et vir   And husband

exception documents   Legible copies of restrictive covenants and documents evidencing exceptions in the commitment (*see* paragraph 6B of the One to Four Family Residential Contract).

exclusions   Items of real or personal property that are not to be included in the conveyance of the property as defined in paragraph 2 of the TREC-promulgated contract forms.

executed contract A contract that has been fully performed. Also used to identify the effective date of the contract when all parties have signed and the offeror has been notified of the acceptance of the offer.

executory contract A contract that is in the process of being performed.

exhibit A document that is attached to a contract to provide documentation supporting something in the principal document; for example, a metes-and-bounds legal description attached to a purchase agreement.

extraterritorial jurisdiction (ETJ) The property located outside of the limits of a municipality that is subject to annexation. The Texas Property Code requires that purchase agreements must contain a statutory notice that property located outside of the city may be in a city's ETJ and subject to annexation.

Fair Housing Act The federal law that prohibits discrimination in housing based on race, color, religion, sex, disability, familial status, and national origin.

femme sole An unmarried woman.

FHA The federal agency under HUD that insures home loans, making loanable funds available to lower income buyers.

fiduciary A legal relationship between two persons who agree that one party will act on behalf of the other party, subject to the principal's direction and control.

forbearance Refraining from taking action.

four corners doctrine The legal requirement that courts interpret the provisions of a contract in the context of the entire agreement; also called the four corners rule.

fraud An act of deceit intended to cause someone to part with money or enter into a contract that he or she would not have entered into if the decision had been based on truth and accurate information.

funding When the seller receives the proceeds from the sale.

funding fee The fee charged by the Department of Veterans Affairs to guarantee a veteran's loan.

general warranty deed The most widely used deed in Texas; a deed that warrants the title free of encumbrances back to the sovereign of the soil. Paragraph 9B of the TREC-promulgated contracts calls for the seller to deliver title at closing by executing and delivering a general warranty deed.

hazard insurance Insurance to indemnify a property owner against financial loss in the event of a casualty loss.

incompetent party One who does not have the legal capacity to enter into a legally binding contract; a minor, or one who is under the influence of alcohol or other mind altering substances, or one who has been declared mentally incompetent by a court.

incomplete construction For purposes of TREC-promulgated forms, a new home that is in the process of being built but is not complete.

informal property description A street address.

improvements Physical additions and fixtures added to land.

intermediary A broker who has been authorized in writing, by the parties to a purchase agreement, to represent both parties following statutory provisions defined in section 1101.559 of the Texas Real Estate License Act.

lawful objective A lawful purpose.

lease A contract that transfers possessory rights from the holder of the fee simple estate to a tenant.

legal description A property description that is of such certainty and accuracy that one can go to it and identify it; a description that is acceptable to the courts; a reference to a recorded plat or a metes-and-bounds description.

lessee The tenant identified in a lease.

lessor The landlord or property owner identified in a lease.

licensee One who holds a valid Texas broker or salesperson license.

license holder One who holds a valid Texas broker or salesperson license.

liquidated damages Monetary damages to be paid by agreement of the parties in the contract when a default occurs.

listing broker The broker who represents the interests of the property owner and acts as the seller's special agent.

mediation A forum in which an impartial person, the mediator, facilitates communication between parties to promote reconciliation, settlement, or understanding.

mineral rights Rights to subsurface land and its profits.

minor A person who has not reached the age of majority and, therefore, does not have legal capacity to transfer title to real property.

MIP *See* mortgage insurance premium.

money damages Monetary damages awarded by a court when a party defaults and causes a financial loss to the nondefaulting party.

mortgage insurance premium (MIP) The cost to purchase the insurance issued by FHA to protect the lender's interest in the event of borrower default (*see* paragraph 12A(2) of the One to Four Family Residential Contract).

mortgagee The lender.

mortgagee's title policy A policy that protects the lender's interest in the event of a failure of title.

mortgagor The borrower.

multiple listing service (MLS) A marketing organization composed of member brokers who agree to share their listing agreements with one another in the hope of procuring ready, willing, and able buyers for their properties more quickly than they could on their own.

mutual agreement A meeting of the minds between parties to a contract when no fraud, misrepresentation, or undue influence has been present in the negotiations.

mutual assent Mutual agreement.

non-realty items Items of personal property that sellers/ buyers might negotiate in the sale of property through the use of the Non-Realty Items Addendum.

notice Information that may be required by the terms of a contract. The effective delivery of notices is defined in paragraph 21 of the TREC-promulgated contract forms.

note A promise to pay.

novation The substitution of a new contract for an existing one or the substitution of a new party to an existing obligation.

offer One of the three components of a valid contract— offer, acceptance, and notification of the acceptance. Offers involving real property interests should always be in writing.

offeree The one to whom the offer is directed.

offeror The one who makes an offer.

option A contractual right that obligates the seller to sell but gives the buyer the unrestricted right to proceed or terminate within a defined time frame and at an agreed upon price. To be valid in Texas, the buyer must deliver valuable consideration (money) to the seller and time is of the essence.

option to purchase A unilateral agreement that binds the property owner and prevents the property owner from selling the property to another party but does not bind the prospective purchaser to purchase.

option to terminate A unilateral agreement that binds the property owner to release the prospective purchaser from all obligations if the buyer elects to walk away during the defined option period.

owner's title policy An insurance policy that indemnifies a property owner against financial loss in the event of a title failure.

parol evidence rule Evidence that is outside and separate from the written contractual agreement and that is not admissible into court.

parties The signatories to a contract.

performance A contractual agreement or promise to do a particular act.

PMI *See* private mortgage insurance.

possession To take occupancy.

prepaids Expense items related to the ownership of a property that are paid in advance, such as loan interest from the date of closing to the first of the next month, the first year's hazard insurance premium plus two additional months to establish the reserve impound account, and the prorated tax amount received from the seller plus an additional two months to be deposited in the reserve impound account.

prevailing party The one who wins in a lawsuit; *see* paragraph 17 of the TREC-promulgated contract forms.

principals The parties to a contract; the buyer and the seller, or the tenant and the landlord.

private mortgage insurance (PMI) The insurance that the borrower must acquire to protect the interest of the lender in the event of borrower default on a greater than 80% LTV-ratio conventional loan (*see* paragraph 12A(2) of the One to Four Family Residential Contract).

promulgated Forms published by the Texas Real Estate Commission for mandatory use by licensees assisting buyers and sellers.

ratification The confirmation of an act already performed.

reasonable time A fair length of time, as determined by the court, for the performance of contractual obligations.

recorded Placed in the public records of the county in which the property is located.

release A document that relieves a person from any further legal obligations.

remedy Something used to correct a wrong.

resale certificate A document issued by a homeowners association that certifies the requirements that the restrictive covenants and association rules impose upon the owner of the property.

rescission The practice of one party canceling or terminating a contract, which has the effect of returning the parties to their original positions before the contract was made.

residential service contract   The statutory name for the contract that limits the owner's financial exposure in the event of a malfunction of the property being purchased; commonly referred to as a home warranty. The companies that issue these contracts are licensed and regulated by the Texas Real Estate Commission.

Real Estate Settlement Procedures Act (RESPA)   A federal law that addresses closing procedures for residential transactions that are financed with a federally related loan.

restrictive covenant   *See* deed restrictions.

rollback tax   A tax that is assessed on Texas property when agriculturally exempted property is converted from agricultural use to another use.

R-value   A measure of insulation. The higher the R-value, the better resistance to the transfer of heat.

sales price   Sum of A, cash portion of the sales price payable by buyer at closing, and B, the sum of all financing.

seller financing   A transaction in which the seller receives part of the consideration as a note secured by a mortgage as part of the consideration. The details of the seller financing are addressed in the TREC Seller Financing Addendum.

seller's agent   The broker representing the seller's interest as a special agent; the listing broker.

seller's expenses   Expenses payable by seller (*see* paragraph 12A(1) of the One to Four Family Residential Contract).

settlement   Closing of the transaction.

short sale   A sale of real estate in which the sale proceeds fall short of the balance owed on the property's mortgage loan.

Statute of Frauds   A state law that requires certain documents and agreements be reduced to writing to be enforceable in a court of law.

subagent   A broker who brings a buyer customer to the real estate transaction.

subdivision   Land that is divided into two or more parcels to be sold separately.

subject to   A clause setting forth any contingencies or special conditions.

surface lease   A lease that addresses rights to the surface of the earth and does not include rights to the air above the property (air rights) or the minerals below the surface (subsurface rights).

survey   The process of determining and measuring land areas and boundaries to identify easements and encroachments.

temporary lease   A leasehold estate that lasts for no more than 90 days.

tenant at sufferance   A tenancy that exists when a party is in possession of the premises after the legal right to occupy those premises has expired.

termination   The act of terminating or bringing to an end. Contract termination may occur by completion of the objective, a change in the law, death or insanity of the parties, expiration, mutual agreement, condemnation or destruction of the property, or bankruptcy of either party.

third party financing   Financing that involves someone other than the seller of the property; may be conventional or government backed.

tidewaters   Waters subject to the changing tides in the Gulf of Mexico.

timber interests   Rights to trees grown for timber that can be negotiated in the sale of a property. Normally growing trees are considered real estate and remain with a property when it sells.

time is of the essence   The contracting parties agree that strict adherence to the time frames recited in the contract is an essential part of their agreement.

timely presentation   Texas real estate licensees are required to present all offers to the client immediately.

title commitment   A document furnished by a title company that establishes the conditions under which the title company will issue an owner's policy of title insurance.

title policy   An owner policy of title insurance (*see* paragraph 6A of the One to Four Family Residential Contract).

tort   An act that damages another individual and gives rise to legal action.

TREC   Texas Real Estate Commission

TRELA   The real estate license act, Chapter 1101 of Texas Occupations Code.

unauthorized practice of law   Engaging in the practice of law by persons or entities not authorized to practice law pursuant to state law. *See* Sec. 1101.654 of TRELA.

unenforceable   A contract that was valid but, for a variety of possible reasons, may no longer be enforced.

unilateral contract   A contract that requires one party to complete a performance before the other party is obligated to act; for example, a seller is not obligated to pay a brokerage fee until the agent produces a ready, willing, and able buyer.

unimproved property   A parcel of land that does not have improvements, fixtures, and accessories.

VA   The Department of Veterans Affairs.

VA-funding fee The fee charged to a veteran by the Department of Veterans Affairs when a VA-guaranteed loan is originated; a fee charged to reduce the cost of administering the VA-loan guarantee program to the American taxpayer.

valid An agreement that meets all of the legal requirements of a contract.

valuable consideration Money.

Vernon's Texas Civil Statutes State laws that do not fall into one of the state's legal codes.

void The absence of something.

voidable A contract that may be set aside at the sole option of one of the contracting parties.

waive To give up or voluntarily surrender a legal right.

warranty A promise or a covenant.

water rights Common law rights held by owners of land adjacent to rivers, lakes, or oceans; includes restrictions on those rights and land ownership.

wetlands Land areas protected by the U.S. government that have groundwater at or near the surface enough of the year to constitute swamps and marshlands.

will An instrument that conveys the real and personal property of a deceased person to a named beneficiary; a devisor conveys a devise (real property) to a devisee.

Answers to Chapter Quizzes and Exercises

Chapter 1 Quiz
1. b
2. c
3. a
4. d
5. d
6. a
7. c
8. b
9. c
10. d

Chapter 2 Quiz
1. c
2. a
3. a
4. b
5. c
6. c
7. c
8. d
9. c
10. d

Chapter 3 Contract Workshop
1. Can the seller terminate on September 28 if he elects to do so? Yes

   On October 3? No, because it is beyond 7 days.

Chapter 3 Quiz
1. b
2. d
3. b
4. d
5. c
6. b
7. d
8. a
9. d
10. c

Chapter 4 Contract Workshop
1. Is the seller obligated to do the repairs? No

   Is the buyer obligated to do the repairs? No
2. Negotiable
3. No. The repairs exceed 5% of the sales price.

Chapter 4 Quiz
1. a
2. b
3. b
4. d
5. c
6. a
7. c
8. c
9. d
10. a

Chapter 5 Contract Workshop
1. Buyer
2. No
3. No
4. Where should the names be on the form? On the right side under Listing Broker

   What should it say in Agreement between Brokers? N/A because there is only one broker
5. Can the buyer terminate the contract? No

   Can the seller terminate the contract? No

   Is the seller obligated to agree? No
6. No
7. Contract is valid; buyer has no option to terminate

Chapter 5 Quiz
1. c
2. b
3. b
4. c
5. d
6. b
7. a
8. d
9. d
10. c

Chapter 6 Quiz
1. d
2. c
3. a
4. b
5. a
6. b
7. d
8. c
9. d
10. c

Chapter 7 Contract Workshop
1. How does the broker satisfy the statutory requirement? It is in paragraph 6E1.
What if a TREC form is not used? It is also in the TAR Buyer/Tenant Representation Agreement and the TREC Notice to Purchaser.
2. September 26
3. No, it is in paragraph 19

Chapter 7 Which Form Do I Use?
1. c
2. f
3. e
4. b
5. g
6. e
7. d
8. e
9. a
10. k
11. j
12. h
13. i
14. l

Chapter 7 True/False Quiz
1. b
2. b
3. a
4. a
5. a
6. b
7. b
8. a
9. b
10. b
11. a
12. b
13. b
14. b
15. b
16. a
17. b
18. a
19. b
20. b

Chapter 7 Quiz
1. b
2. a
3. b
4. d
5. a
6. d
7. c
8. b
9. d
10. a

Chapter 8 Review Questions
1. d
2. d
3. d
4. a
5. d
6. d
7. c
8. b
9. a
10. d

Index

Notes

Notes

Notes

Notes

Notes

Notes

Notes

Notes

Notes

Notes

Notes

Notes